My Home Has Wheels— Please Move Me

by

Susan R. Henley

DORRANCE PUBLISHING CO., INC.
PITTSBURGH, PENNSYLVANIA 15222

The contents of this work including, but not limited to, the accuracy of events, people, and places depicted; opinions expressed; permission to use previously published materials included; and any advice given or actions advocated are solely the responsibility of the author, who assumes all liability for said work and indemnifies the publisher against any claims stemming from publication of the work.

All Rights Reserved
Copyright © 2012 by Susan R. Henley

No part of this book may be reproduced or transmitted, downloaded, distributed, reverse engineered, or stored in or introduced into any information storage and retrieval system, in any form or by any means, including photocopying and recording, whether electronic or mechanical, now known or hereinafter invented without permission in writing from the publisher.

Dorrance Publishing Co., Inc.
701 Smithfield Street
Pittsburgh, PA 15222
Visit our website at www.dorrancebookstore.com

ISBN: 978-1-4349-2821-4
eISBN: 978-1-4349-2173-4

Acknowledgement

To All My Readers:

First of all, I want everyone to know it was my wife's idea to write this book. The more she wrote, the better I liked what I read. The facts in this book are all basically true, except for a few name changes.

I am the son of a sharecropper. I do only have a sixth grade education. But from the time I was old enough to remember, I had a dream. I dreamed of having a small business of my own—being my own boss. I also dreamed of having a small farm, to a sort, and owning, raising, and showing registered quarter horses.

With a lot of hard work, I was able to do all of these things and more. The point of this book is to let you know that if you have enough willpower and a dream, and set your mind to it, anything is possible.

This book does not come close to telling all my true stories and experiences. I chose only to tell some of those that meant the most to me. Some of the funny stories still make me laugh. Some of the stories of the bad times still make me want to cry. I hope that they will all touch you in much of the same way they have me in molding my life.

So many young people today start to do something. And because they encounter obstacles or difficulty, they quit. I would sincerely hope that if you read this book, it will encourage you to keep on trying and always follow your dream. Being poor, not having the best education, or even misfortune should never be an excuse for not following your dream. Part of my success in life was not ever quitting, even when it looked impossible to overcome the very worst of hard times.

If only one person, young or old, whatever age, reads my story and is inspired by my true experiences, bad and good alike, to continue toward his or her dream and succeeds, I will have accomplished far more than my own success!

Sincerely,

Bobby Henley
Mobile Home Transporter

My Home Has Wheels—Please Move Me
True Experiences of a Mobile Home Mover

Phillips County, Arkansas, at the foot of Crowley's Ridge, is where my story begins. Being the first son of a sharecropper in the poorest county in the state will never be my greatest regret. Farming is a tireless, thankless way to make a living or working for some, who, most of the time, treated their workers less than a human. It's a demeaning way to make a living. Daddy would drive the tractor from sunup until long after sundown while we older kids chopped cotton along with the adults. In the fall, instead of going to school, we would pick cotton until our fingers would bleed from pulling cotton from the prickly bolls.

  We were grateful for our living quarters for what they were even though they were just run-down tenant shacks with no running water and with holes on the floors. In order to keep away the mice, rats, snakes, and any other varmint that might scurry in, we used Prince Albert cans, old rusty lids, or anything else we could find and nailed them over the holes to keep the critters out. At bath time, we kids would draw up water from a well and carry bucketsful to a large metal tub on the porch. My younger brothers, who always seemed to be covered in dirt from head to toe, would get scrubbed down first in that tub. By the time my older sister and I got to bathe in that same tub of water, it was filthy with a floating layer of grime and soap combined. I hated crawling in that nasty water and taking my bath. I knew it was either bale in that tub or suffer the consequences from Mama, who insisted we clean up.

In order to feed our large family, we grew fruit and vegetables and raised animals to supplement the family until the owner of the farm gave us our wages. It was an exciting day when we could go to the mercantile in town and buy the flour, lard, sugar, and other staples so Mama would be able to feed this large family. Mama stretched out those kitchen staples as far as she could, and when we ran out, we did without until the next furnish was due. It was our way of life and we accepted it, for that was the way it was. That is for everyone but me! I kept telling Daddy and Mama that there had to be a better way. From the time I was old enough to chop cotton, I worked as hard as a grown-up to put as much cotton in that tow sack as the old hands working beside me. I knew I had to work hard, so when I was big enough to reach the gears and sit on those old tractor seats, I could plow as well as Daddy. I knew there would be a better life out there for me. My whole family called me a dreamer and ridiculed me, saying the poor will always be poor and the rich will just get richer. This is our life and that's how it is. But deep in my soul, I always knew my life would somehow be different, if only I believed it.

The first glimpse of my future life appeared when I quit school after an incident in the sixth grade. On that fateful day, I wore blue jeans to school that had patches on the seat. When the teacher called on me to go write on the blackboard, one of those patches had come loose and the whole classroom burst into laughter. I went home and told my Daddy that I was never going back to school again; the embarrassment was more than I could bear. It wasn't just that incident, but many others before, that had sealed my fate. He threatened to whip me and take me to school, but I stood my ground. I told him he could whip me every day, but I was never going back to school again and be ridiculed because I was poor. Soon after, the first big change into my future came out of nowhere. One of those rich farmers let me prove my ability to succeed. He let me drive that tractor and plow those fields like a grown man. When he came by to check my work and saw my rows long and straight, he agreed to pay me more money than my Daddy. No one in my family, including Daddy or my uncles, was making that much money. I guess you could say I knew there was a glimmer of hope for a better life.

I worked hard to prove myself each day. I watched and learned from the adults around me. I told myself that if they can do it, so can I. I was eager to learn, and the farmer I worked for noticed something in me from the start. He asked me of things that no child should be able to accomplish, but I tried hard until I got it right. Here in the South, the old-timers called it "grit in your craw." I had so much grit in my craw and desire to have a better life. I should have had a chaffed rear end.

I saved my money, and my uncles on the farm were jealous when I came back from town with brand new Levi blue jeans with no patches on the rear end and new shirts that weren't handed down from someone else. My desire to have a better life had really begun. I could see my path to a better life as plain as day. I was changing my way of life. This is the beginning of all the experiences that will be shared by a son of a sharecropper farmer with a sixth grade education from the poorest county in Arkansas at the foot of Crowley's Ridge.

I have changed my life just like I always knew I could. I have become successful by working hard, being honest, and treating everyone the way in which I would want to be treated. I move people's mobile homes on wheels down our highways. Stop and think about it. I know some of you have seen that long metal home being towed beside your car or truck on the highway. Were you the courteous driver who moved over for me so I could safely pass or were you the one with your arm out the window shaking your fist at me to move out of your way? Whichever one you may be, I hope some of my true experiences in this book will bring a smile to your face as I share my stories in the life of a mobile home mover.

Chapter One

Yosemite Sam and I Get Started

From 1964 to mid 1982, I had tried a little bit of everything, hoping to improve my life. I toiled from daylight till after dusk for several farmers, and then worked for a dirt plant in England, Arkansas. I was a line supervisor at a factory that built Jacuzzi pumps, and then was an overseer for a cattle operation in Scott, Arkansas with several hundred head of heifers with calves. I bought and traded farm equipment with a rice and soybean farmer, and then went into a custom hay baling business with my brother. I made a decent living at all of these jobs, but nothing ever seemed to fit what I had in mind for my life. I still knew I wanted something more.

My brother went to work for a land developer in 1982. Our hay baling business was good for only a few months of the year, and we weren't making ends meet. One morning, my brother called and said, "You're not doing anything today. Come and go to work with me."

I decided he was right. It was a slow time for me, and I would go along just to beat the boredom. I worked with him part time and picked up a few extra bucks. The land developer liked my work and offered me a full-time job. He soon realized that my experience working on the farm had given me a knack for running equipment. Before long, I was clearing lots in his subdivision with a bulldozer and backhoe, preparing them for sale for mobile homes he bought and sold. By then, the land developer had bought his own mobile home toter truck, and my brother was pulling them faster than we could get the lots ready.

Now, before you dash to your computer and Google, like a friend of mine did, let me explain what a toter truck is. A mobile home toter truck is an eighteen-wheeler that has a shortened frame and has one of the back axles and rear tires removed. A hydraulic hitch, with a ball that moves up and down and sideways, is permanently mounted to the rear of the truck. This ball hooks to the tongue of a mobile home in the same way a hitch on your car or truck connects to your boat trailer or camper to pull it down the road. I felt you needed to know this because my toter truck is how I will make my living for the next thirty plus years.

Now, my boss never minded asking anyone to jump right in and do whatever needed to be done. He was impatient. And when he wanted something, he wanted it done right now. He soon told me that I was going to have to help my brother and the mobile home crew to get some of these homes set up and ready for moving into. I had never set up a mobile home before, but I knew that if I wanted to keep this job, I better be a quick learner. With him, it was always his way or the highway!

The mobile home business was booming. People were buying mobile homes, and the lots were selling like hot cakes. We had more work than we could get done in a day or week. My boss had us working fourteen to sixteen hours a day, six days a week to keep up. Now, you know I'm not afraid of hard work and I have a huge desire to make money to improve my life, but I flatfootedly refused to work for my boss on Sunday. By refusing to work on Sunday, I thought this would be the end of this job, but when everyone on the crew refused to work on Sunday along with me, I knew I would still have a paycheck.

Life at home had not been good for a while. My first wife was a good woman, but she just never wanted the things out of life that I did. She was perfectly happy to go to work each day and come home. As long as the bills got paid, she was content. But I just wasn't happy with my life! It's hard to work like I did and not have a partner to support your dreams. I still wanted so much more in life. I'm telling you this not to put her down, but to let you know how I met my present wife, Susan.

My brother and I pulled up the office one morning and got out ready to go to work. I had seen this girl at the office every day, but I only had work on my mind. I hardly ever went into the office. I just came to work and went back home each day. I asked my brother, "Who is that girl?"

He replied, "That's the boss's secretary and bookkeeper, Susan. She writes our checks. Don't ever piss her off! She's been working for the boss for fifteen years."

Now, all work and no play makes for a dull boy! I found myself looking for more reasons to go into that office from that day on. Once I got in that office, I didn't want to leave anytime soon. Susan was really fun to talk to, and I found myself flirting more and more with her. If she will tell the truth, she flirted back, too. By the time my wife and I split up, Susan and I were already close to each other. We would eat lunch together and talk about anything together. We both were hard workers and wanted some of the same things in life. Without even knowing what was happening, we were forming a personal and business bond that would grow into our future destiny. No decisions in the mobile home business were ever made again without her and me discussing it first.

In late 1983, the Texas and Oklahoma oil crunch hit. The U.S. went into a recession and all the mobile home finance companies quit offering mobile home financing. Hundreds of folks were losing their jobs in the south and letting their mobile homes be repossessed. Everywhere we went, mobile homes were sitting abandoned and vacant. A representative from the finance company, with whom my boss did business, came to visit him. We had been pulling a few repos in for him for a while, but now the situation had become very grave.

He told my boss he had a proposal and needed his help. He wanted someone who would go and get those repossessed mobile homes sitting around the state and store them in one central location. He would pay him to bring them in, clean them up, repair them, and pay a commission to resell them. Now, my boss had a real knack for sniffing out where the opportunity of making money comes from. He saw huge dollar signs immediately, and, after very little thought, became the repo lot for that finance company.

Requests came in on several repossessions every day. With one truck, there was no way to provide the finance company with speedy results. My boss called my brother and me into the office and told us that we needed to look for another mobile home toter truck. He didn't want the responsibility of another truck and suggested that we buy it ourselves. He would pay us for pulls our truck made. That way we could all make more money, plus keep the finance company happy.

My brother and I didn't have much money saved back, but we talked it over and liked the idea. However, we didn't know how to make this opportunity happen. I started looking at toter trucks, but most of the mobile home toters were priced way out of our means, and we were skeptical about this idea really working. As luck would have it, I ran into a friend of mine who knew about a 1965 International toter truck for sale. He told me that he thought it could be bought for around 2,000 dollars. Now, we're talking about a twenty-year-old truck and that seemed like an awful lot of money for an old truck, but I knew it was worth looking into. When I drove up to look at the truck, it *looked* like a twenty-year-old truck, and I figured at first glance it certainly had seen better days. When it started right up, I thought maybe it was worth a shot. I took it for a test drive and there seemed to be very little wrong with it mechanically. Maybe just a few weathered hoses or belts, an oil change, and new tires. I'd worked on all kinds of old junk equipment for years on the farm and kept those machines going. Why not try it with this old truck?

But one thing made me step back and think about how crazy this was. On both doors of this twenty-year-old truck, someone apparently with a great sense of humor had painted huge colorful images of "Yosemite Sam." I'm not talking about small little decals, I'm talking about Yosemite Sam (pistols at his hip, spurs on his boots, with full cowboy hat and mustache) in full color, about three feet tall, on both doors. I kept asking myself, *Was I really going to drive this truck down the road, all over the state, pulling mobile homes with Yosemite Sam at my side? I'd already suffered a lot of ridicule in my life, but was I really ready for what I knew would come from this?* Oh, well, what the heck, maybe I would give it a try. And 1,700 dollars later, Yosemite Sam and I became "pardners."

I told you that my boss wanted us to buy another truck, but when Yosemite Sam and I drove up to work that first morning, I wasn't really sure this would work. My boss loved to make money, but he didn't really want to share too much with others. I don't think he really thought my brother and I would have the money to buy our own truck. In fact, he was mad about the whole thing at first, but his need to keep the finance company happy soon outweighed his greed. We came to a verbal agreement about how he would pay us for the pulls Yosemite Sam and I made, and my pardner and I were officially in the mobile home transport business.

That 1,700 dollars invested in Yosemite Sam was a lot of money for my brother and me. We formed Henley Trucking so we could keep tract of what we made. After two weeks of driving Yosemite Sam and pulling repo mobile homes, we took our invoices to the boss to collect our pay. We were so proud and excited that this might work out because our invoices for two weeks totaled over 6,000 dollars. Then my boss dropped his bombshell on us. He had not collected from the finance company and could not pay us until they paid him. Now, my brother and I had scraped the bottom of the barrel for fuel, oil, and permits to pull those repos and we were busted. I was disheartened and mad, too. I told the boss that it wasn't our agreement, and I needed my money. He went back into the office and sent Susan out with a check for 500 dollars. What the hell would that help? It wouldn't even pay for the fuel I had paid out. I got mad and drove off, thinking what a big mistake I had made this time.

At this point, my brother was still working for the boss, driving his toter truck. And he needed this job, so he kept on working. I was too stubborn and proud-hearted to go back until we got our money. For a week, I called every day asking to collect my money, but the boss kept telling me he just didn't have any money yet. Finally, after a week of kicking myself in the butt, Susan called and told me that the boss had gotten a check from the finance company. She said that if I wanted my money, I had better get there before he would spend it. She became my inside source of when and how to collect my money. After all those fifteen years with the boss, she did hold a lot of influence with him, and, as I told you before, she and I had really became close.

Reluctantly, I might add, I drove to the office, and the boss had Susan write me a check for my invoices in full. I was still mad at the way he had treated me, but I finally had my money in hand. As luck would have it, the man from the finance company was there that same morning, and he, my brother, Susan, and I had become friends while forming a good business relationship. After the boss left to check on a crew, we all sat visiting in the office. The finance man unfortunately had heard the whole conversation with the boss about paying me my money. He was laughing and teasing me about Yosemite Sam. He said, "Do you think you and Sam can make it to Texas with some repos? I'll pay you good money to pull them to a dealer in Sulphur Springs, Texas." Now, Sam had really been reliable up to this point, but I wasn't sure about taking him all the way to Texas. But then I thought, *Why not?*

Well, Sam and I made about twenty trips to Texas without a hitch, and the best part was every time I delivered a repo to that dealer, he would come out smiling with a check in his hand for my hard work. Now, I was really walking in tall cotton. Sam and I had become interstate mobile home transporters, and my brother and I couldn't have been prouder of our investment.

The boss was getting farther and farther behind getting those repos pulled in by the time Sam and I finished our Texas trips. He begged me to come back to work and help him, but I still remembered how badly he treated me about my money. Reluctantly, I agreed, but I told him I would never argue about my money with him again. I had money in the bank from my Texas trips, and we finally agreed that I would wait to be paid until he collected each time. But when he collected from the finance company, I would be paid! I knew now that Susan would keep me informed when the checks come in.

Yosemite Sam and I worked hard, but he was still a twenty-year-old truck. I treated that old truck with all the respect and care it deserved. But after pulling it out of retirement, it was like an old man. Things were starting to quit and shut down. It was beginning to need regular quarts of oil, and the parking brake was totally gone. But Sam kept pulling those repos.

One of the last experiences Sam and I had, before I decided to retire that old truck, came when the boss sent a man named Bob and I to Wye Mountain to get a repo one morning. Bob was a scraggly little man with a beard who wouldn't weigh 140 pounds. He was soaking wet carrying two eight-inch concrete blocks under each arm. Now, this particular repo was sitting on a huge slope, and we both knew it would be tricky for Sam to get it off the lot. And remember, I told you that Sam's parking brake was totally gone, so we had to scotch the wheels of that old truck so it wouldn't roll off. We backed Sam's hitch up to the tongue of that repo and started getting it ready. I hollered at Bob to make sure he had scotched the wheels of Sam really tight, so we could get started.

Bob hollered back, "It's scotched just fine. Jack up the home and get those blocks out."

After jacking that repo up about three inches, I looked up, and Sam's hitch had come loose from the tongue of that repo and was rolling down that slope. I looked up just in time to see all 140 pounds of Bob running beside Sam, trying to grab the door handle and pull himself into that old truck. The more Bob ran, the faster Sam's speed got going downhill. When Bob realized that Sam was getting away from him, the next thing he did was grab hold of Sam by his front bumper, holding on for dear life. I was laughing so hard watching Sam bounce Bob around like a string, hanging on with each bump they hit. Finally, I hollered at Bob, "Let go of that damn old truck before it runs over, you fool."

Bob let go, and, as Sam reached the bottom of that hill, it hit a small ditch and turned enough to slow Sam down. Sam just rested there, gently rocking back and forth unharmed. I made sure that Bob was okay, except maybe he needed to change his pants. Slowly, we walked down the hill, and there was Sam still purring like a kitten waiting for us to bring him back up that hill. We both scotched those wheels this time and brought that repo back to the lot. But I knew Yosemite Sam had served me well, and it was nearly time to look for a more reliable mobile home toter truck. I hated to get rid of Sam. He had served me well and given me a start in the mobile home business, but Yosemite Sam was due for his full retirement.

Chapter Two

Homes, Inc.—Good Times

My boss had sold mobile homes and had been a land developer for more years than I am old. He should have been a millionaire several times over, but he could not hold on to his money. His biggest downfall was his love of women, and he liked to impress them. Believe me, there were a lot of women to impress. At this time, he had a woman in his life (unknown to his wife of nearly fifty years) who loved my boss's money. I remember one particular day they had been shopping. When I walked into the office, she was showing off the ten pairs of shoes he had bought her. She was trying on those shoes and modeling them for us all. Susan had seen more of this in her fifteen years of working for him than I had, but this woman had such a strong hold on the boss that the two of them would carry on like dogs in heat and never tried to hide it from anyone. This woman really had her claws in the old man. When the finance man came around to check the repos on our lot, she would be beside the boss the whole time. It sickened us to watch all this because then he would have Susan rip three or four checks out of the checkbook and take this woman shopping for whatever she wanted. And she wanted it all. It was his business and his money, but it was apparent it would soon affect our paychecks.

Not long after this, he moved a double-wide mobile home in for her to live in (their private little love nest, or so they thought), but his wife found out. She raised hell and created all sorts of havoc by changing their plans. Yet, at one point, I really believed he would leave his wife for this other woman.

Why he brought Susan and I into this mess, I'll never know, but he questioned us on what he should do. We both knew that this woman had a strong hold on him, but we had no intention in getting involved any more than we already were with this messy situation. It was going to have to be his decision. The finance man had been around a lot during this time also and knew this was headed for a catastrophe if something wasn't done quickly. By then, he knew that Susan was basically running the office while the boss played, and my brother and I were doing the hard work with crews to keep the money flowing in. He finally called a meeting with my brother, myself, Susan, and Beverly (Susan's assistant). He told us he could see that lightning was going to strike soon, and he had thought of a plan to head it off before a disaster occurred. He said, "Let me talk to the old man first and see if I can convince him that this plan will work, and then I'll tell you what I have in mind."

After several hours of meeting with the boss, we were all brought in to talk about this new plan of action. I still don't know to this day how he convinced the boss to buy it, but however he did it, I will always be thankful. I think he may have given him an ultimatum to either work it out or he would take the finance business elsewhere.

His proposal was to form a new company with my brother, myself, Susan, Beverly, and the boss as equal partners in the new corporation. The boss would be a silent partner with no check signing privileges, but he would reap any profits made just like the rest of us. We four would be in total operating control of the repossessed home operation, which by now had snowballed into a real mess.

In the next few days, we filed our corporation papers, forming Homes, Inc. I would be the president, my brother would be the vice president, Susan would be the secretary, Beverly would be the treasurer, and the boss would be a silent shareholder. None of us had much money, but we managed to open a checking account and put enough money together to operate for about thirty days. All five of us agreed not to draw a paycheck from the company until a check for pulling repos in for the finance company arrived in about thirty days.

We managed to pay all the help, make payments on the toter truck (which the boss made a part of our deal, including the remaining payments owed on it), pay our fuel expense, and keep the lights and water on in the office. That's about all we did, though. We literally were all counting change in the last few days before that first check arrived from the finance company. When Beverly checked the mail and that first check had finally arrived, we all breathed a sigh of relief, and knew things would be better. We each finally got a paycheck from *our* new corporation! Now, things really started working in our favor, but not so much for the finance company. No longer could we keep up with the steady flow of repos they were sending us, so we decided to buy another toter truck. We found a 1983 Brigadier that had been converted to a toter truck that would work. By then, we had hired a young man named Robby who had a little experience pulling mobile homes. We had a Mexican man who was a top hand to help, and we put him in the other company truck to pull in. Yosemite Sam and I were still plugging along, but just barely. He and I would do only the short distance repos to the lot because I knew he was on his last leg. I knew the time had come to retire Sam. The hinges on his doors were rusty and barely hanging on, and we were an accident waiting for a place to happen. The time had come to say "Good-bye, Sam."

On another note regarding trucks, I remember one day in particular when I had just backed my repo into a slot on the sales lot and was walking toward the office. When I turned and looked up the road, I saw Robby barreling down Highway 111 toward our lot with his repo, black smoke pouring from underneath. He had run off a tire just up the road and kept on going because he was so close. Apparently, the sparks from the rim of that tire had caught some of the hanging insulation on fire and was blazing. We all ran across the lot and hurried him to stop and began pulling the burning debris from under the repo. Flames were already running up the side of the mobile home and had begun to singe the paint off the metal siding. Luckily, we were able to get the flames put out. In a huge heap lay the singed and smoldering insulation beside it. I asked him what the heck he thought he was doing. His reply was, "Boss, I didn't know I was on fire."

How can you pull a mobile home down the road with black smoke billowing and flames shooting up the side and not notice? My heart was beating a 100 miles an hour, and, with a few more minutes of pulling that mobile home down the highway, our whole business with the finance company would have been in jeopardy. As far as Homes, Inc. was concerned, his career was finished with our company.

The Homes, Inc. sales lot was by now packed full of repos from the finance company. It was a full-time job to just clean them, repair them, and resell them. My brother was put in charge of a crew to get them ready to sell, while the rest of the crews kept dragging them in.

Now, I don't think most of you have a good picture of what a repossessed mobile home looks like. Some folks have to face the fact that they have lost their job, have no money, and would quietly gather their personal belongings and abandon their mobile homes. Those are the repossessions we like to go after because sometimes they didn't need much work to make them suitable for selling. But that was not the normal situation. A lot of people were depressed and angry about the situation they were in, and unfortunately took their frustration out on that mobile home. They kicked holes in the walls and ripped bedroom and bathroom doors off the hinges, jerked lights and fans off the ceiling, and sometimes would even steal the kitchen sink and bathtubs. Most of the time, they would take the stove, refrigerator, dishwasher, and central air unit. Now, that was mortgaged property, but I always felt like they thought it was the least they deserved for the few years they had paid on that mobile home, with the finance company. Not only that, those items would bring some quick money if sold.

Then there are the repos, and folks thought how nice it would be to leave us "presents" behind, like food left in the refrigerator. With no electricity, the flies were drawn to this rotting mess and laid their eggs. And of course, these hatched out maggots were as big as your fingers. Tropical fish were also left behind, floating in a mess of slimy, green rot. Not only is it an inhumane thing to do to the repo people who have to clean this all up, but to leave a living, breathing thing to die of starvation is cruel. Dog and cat feces stomped and ground into carpeting as they made their exit with only the stuff they could grab and go with in a hurry. Even toilets packed full of human feces, paper, and urine because—oh, yeah—the utility company shut the water off before they could vacate this mobile home. And since most mobile homes were located out in the county, don't forget the animals we have found inside and out over the years. Dogs, cats, rats, squirrels, birds, snakes, ferrets, and even a horse one time that I don't know how it got in that mobile home. I promise you, this is only part of the truth of the conditions I have experienced in the repo mobile home business over the years. Are you starting to get the picture in your mind of what my job has been like? Those repos are a nasty job, but someone had to do it, and it paid me very well.

That's when I went into major debt big time for my second toter truck. The corporation didn't have anymore money or credit, so it was up to me to get financed personally. The truck was a 1986 International—a sharp brown color with blue stripes and less than 80,000 miles. So after I signed several lines for 36,000 dollars at 1,300 dollars per month for three years, I finally had a good dependable truck to drive. Over the next twenty-five years, "Brownie" would make this poor country boy from Phillips County a ton of money.

Now remember, we are in a mild recession, work was slim for a lot of boys who had been in the mobile home business many more years than I had. When we start pulling repo mobile homes down every pig trail in Arkansas with three trucks every day, those other mobile home boys were starting to pay close attention to Homes, Inc. They would be at the fuel station every morning, drinking coffee when we would pull up with three toter trucks and three escort trucks while preparing for our day's work.

Now, I know what most of you are thinking about now. What the heck is an escort truck? Escort trucks are the pickups you see in front of those mobile homes with yellow flashing lights, yellow and black wide load signs, and bright red stick flags waving above. We've got to warn all travelers on the roads with us to get over out of our way somehow. Day in and day out, when those six trucks would fuel up, those boys couldn't believe we were out there working, especially when they were still sitting, drinking coffee when we drove off, waiting for their company to call with work. And when they had work, they would come pass Homes, Inc. trucks everywhere they went. The talk was out in the mobile home business in Arkansas. Those folks at Homes, Inc. must know something their companies didn't because their trucks were burning up the road pulling mobile homes, and, at every turn, they saw Homes, Inc. trucks. Susan started getting calls at the office from other company mobile home drivers. They wanted a piece of the action for some of them were starving, just trying to keep their head above water in the mobile home business.

Homes, Inc. was now selling those repos faster than we could pull them to the lot and get them ready. I would pull repos in each day, and Susan and I would stay at that office till dark, seven days a week, showing homes to buyers. The finance man sent a mobile home dealer from Missouri who owned five sales lots to look at repos. I spent most of that day climbing in and out of those homes. And at the end of the day, he made an offer to buy forty repos at once. The next day, his offer was approved, and I called him back.

The first question he asked was, "How fast can you pull these homes to Missouri?"

I knew that with just three trucks it would take time, but I told him we would start the next day.

Susan and I had a feeling that if we could provide excellent service, this would turn into good money for Homes, Inc. It was time for Homes, Inc. to expand our operation in order to keep up with this growing business. One morning, I was at the fuel station, and a driver from Texas was there fueling up his toter truck with a repo in tow. He looked at me from the pump beside him and said, "I'm so sick of this mobile home business I could vomit. If I could find anyone with money, I'd sell this truck and walk back to Texas!"

I turned to him and asked, "How much money would you need to sell your old truck?"

He replied, "If anyone had 10,000 dollars, I'd sign over the title to them."

He was dead serious. I drove the truck and gave it a good going over. I then called Susan at the office and told her to contact the bank to get a cashier's check for 10,000 dollars because I just bought us another truck. I paid the boy, and we bought him a bus ticket back home. We even drove him to the bus station before he changed his mind. That's the honest truth.

My brother, who was becoming jealous of all my traveling, had a truck to drive of his own again. We then leased in two drivers, Larry and Dave, from the other mobile home transport company to work for us. To keep things moving smoothly, we four partners sat down and discussed how to manage the drivers and trucks. My brother and the Mexican would stay here and pull repos to the lot. Larry, Dave, and I would take those homes to Benton, Poplar Bluff, and Sikeston, Missouri. That dealer was selling those repos as fast as we could pull them to his lots. Everyone was making money with Homes, Inc., including two new lease drivers and the dealer in Missouri. The dealer came back two more trips and bought thirty to forty more repos.

About this same time, a well-known mobile home tycoon and acquaintance called the office, asking for me. I was gone, of course, but when I walked in later, Susan told me who had called.

I asked her, "What did *he* want with *me*?"

Susan said, "Something about buying nearly 500 repos in Texas in one place, some finance company's repo portfolio. He wants our help."

I was really puzzled and wondered how I could possibly help this man, who I knew was worth a lot of money. I contacted him, and he told me the whole story. He had borrowed the money to buy these repos, and interest on his loan would be astronomical. He wanted to know if I knew anyone who might be able to buy some of the repos from him quickly to cut down the amount of his loan. The whole time we were talking, I was thinking about the dealer in Missouri, who had sold a large part of the repos he had bought from Homes, Inc. Besides, I didn't have many on hand right now to spare. I told him to give me a few days, and I would work on it.

The next day, I called my dealer in Missouri and told him about all the repos I had found in one location. He was immediately excited and wanted to know when he could look at them, how much they cost, and where they were. I told him that they were all stored at an old airfield in Texas, and, if he was interested, he and I could meet and check it out. We made plans to meet two days later in Texas. He arrived in his private plane, and I drove down there to meet him. For three days, we jumped in and out of repos, with him making extensive notes of size, serial numbers, and the condition of homes that might interest him. I helped him all I could because I knew that whatever he bought there, my Homes, Inc. trucks would get to pull them to Missouri.

At the end of this, he flew back to Missouri with his notes, and I took my tired butt home to Arkansas, where Susan was waiting to find out what had transpired in Texas. I told her that I didn't really know yet, but I had a really good feeling from the dealer that he might buy quite a few homes. We both had high hopes that he would call the next week.

On Monday morning, the dealer called, asking how many homes he could buy. I asked him point blank, "How many do you want to buy?"

He replied, "Depending on the price, as many as the man will sell me!"

Now keep up! With my next phone call, I arranged for a meeting with the mobile home tycoon, my dealer, and myself for the next day at his office in Conway. Susan and I arrived at the airport and waited for his plane to land, and I was nervous as a cat on a hot tin roof. After arriving, my dealer, Susan, and I drove to the tycoon's office to begin our negotiations. Within three hours, my dealer had taken his checkbook out and written the tycoon a check for 100 totally refurbished repos at 6,000 dollars each and 220 more at 2,700 dollars each. We all shook hands on the deal, and when I dropped him off at the Conway Airport, he looked at Susan and I and said, "I'll fax you a complete list tomorrow and let you know which homes to pull to which of my sales lots. Thank you both so much. I think we've made a good deal."

Made a Good Deal! Susan and I knew this would be one of those deals of a lifetime for us and Homes, Inc.

Our phone was already ringing when we got back to the office. The mobile home tycoon was calling. He told me, "My friend, you have saved my life. This deal more than cleared what I paid for the whole shebang. For every ten repos your dealer bought, I'm going to let you buy one refurbished repo for 5,000 dollars, if you want them. And I'm indebted to you forever. If you ever need a favor from me…call."

Little did we both know, at the time, that I would have to call in that favor a couple of years down the road.

We leased in four more trucks and drivers to handle this deal. For nearly eight months, we pulled repos to our dealer in Missouri. Each Friday, either my brother or I, depending on who delivered last, would walk into that dealer's office, and he would write a check in full for our week's pulls. I kept thinking, *It just doesn't get any better than this.*

Toward the end of pulling those repos to Missouri, I was in Texas hooking my truck, Brownie, to the tongue of one of these homes when a man walked up and introduced himself. He had noticed Homes, Inc. trucks hooking up to several homes, and I guess one of my drivers directed him to me as the boss.

He said, "Do you pull homes for anybody or just your own?"

I grinned really big and said, "Sir, we pull for dead presidents."

He started laughing and said, "Well, son, I understand that concept, and I can accommodate you if you can pull forty homes I just bought to Florida."

I told him to call Susan at the office and get a price per home from her. Also, I'd see what we could do, but I had a few more I had to pull to Missouri first.

Susan gave him a price, and he agreed we were more than fair, but he wanted them in Florida before the Christmas holidays, which was only a few weeks away. We weren't going to turn him down, and I told him we would give it our best shot. That next weekend, Larry, Dave, and I drove from Missouri back to Texas, and the Mexican and my brother, plus the other driver, left Arkansas and met us there.

When we first met that first afternoon at the repo storage lot, it was an unseasonably hot day in December, and so sultry that you couldn't get a good breath. The wind was beginning to pick up, and the air was filling with dust and small bits of debris. I looked up to the southwest and saw that a tornado had formed and was heading straight for us all. I grabbed my CB radio microphone and hollered to all my drivers, "There's a tornado headed this way, take cover immediately!"

But in south Texas the land lay flat and wide open. Where could we go? I jumped in Brownie and prayed really hard. By then, I couldn't see anyone or anything. Mobile homes were being flipped over; metal sidings, shingles, and debris were flying through the air.

Although it seemed like an eternity before it was over, in reality, I knew the tornado lasted only a few minutes, if not just a few seconds before it passed and everything was calm again. I had no idea what had happened to everyone. Did they find shelter, or were they injured or had died? When voices started coming in over the CB radios, I couldn't believe what I heard. Everyone was safe, although they were badly shaken from the ordeal. Also and quite remarkably, all our mobile homes were okay. I looked up at the clearing skies and said, "Thank you, Lord. God takes care of those who try the hardest."

We got ourselves together and pulled those repos to Florida, and we were ready to leave with the last ones on December 22. I called Susan to get our Louisiana permits faxed to the motel and she told me, "You are all about screwed. It's supposed to be pouring down rain in south Louisiana, and you will never make it home for Christmas."

Susan and I have a blended family, and together, we have seven children. Christmas is a big deal at our house. It took me a while to call Susan and tell her what happened because I knew she would be afraid I wasn't telling her the whole truth. Finally, I found the courage and somehow convinced her that everyone and everything would be all right, and I promised her that we would make it back by Christmas Eve. But I knew in my heart that she would cry if I didn't make it back. I would be in big trouble, but this was our last load to Florida, and I wanted to be done with it and go home.

One of my drivers had an escort driver whose CB handle was Joker. He was always pulling pranks on everyone, and this is how he earned his CB handle. He had been to the scale house on I-20 coming out of Texas and had made friends with the scale officer. He asked the scale officer what he wanted Santa Claus to bring him for Christmas. The officer replied, "Oh, my, I don't need anything, but I sure like a good whiskey over the holidays."

Now, when it rains in Louisiana, you *don't* pull mobile homes, you do not move, you do not pass go! To add to all these, two days before Christmas, it was flooding in south Louisiana.

I didn't want to call Susan and tell her we probably weren't going to make it home. I knew she would cry and that's the last thing I would want to do to her right before Christmas. But Joker came to the rescue that day. He rolled into the scale house and carried that scale officer two gallons of the best whiskey he could buy. I really think that scale officer's name could have been St. Nick. He told Joker that if we wanted to ease on out of those scales and take our chances, he might just turn his head the other way for a while. We pulled across the whole state of Louisiana without a hitch and delivered in Destin, Florida the next day. The whole crew was able to spend the holidays with their families, just like it should be. We all needed a break and took a whole week off from Christmas until after the New Year. All the lease drivers knew that the big deals were over and were worried we wouldn't have enough work for them. We told them that we still had a few homes left to pull for the dealer in Missouri, but after that, times might be slow. After all, it was winter, and it's hard to pull mobile homes in rain, sleet, and snow.

After Christmas was over and I pulled the last repos into the dealer's lot in Missouri, he motioned me into his office and wanted to know how many states Homes, Inc. was licensed to transport mobile homes. I told him, "Nearly all of them in the continental U.S."

He asked if we would like to try and pull some of his new mobile homes from several factories in Alabama and Mississippi to his five lots. I asked him about how many homes he was talking about, and his estimate was thirty to forty per month. My heart started thumping, and I had dollar signs dancing across my mind. With the repo business and these additional new hauls, it might just keep us going.

When I got home, I guess I had the grin of a Cheshire cat because, by then, Susan and I were really close, and she knew me pretty well. I was always dead tired after pulling one of those repos for 300 miles to Missouri and 300 miles back. All I usually wanted to do was eat a good home cooked meal and relax, so I could start out again the next day. When I told her what the dealer had proposed, we both knew that the Good Lord would take care of our family, and if things went well, all our drivers', escorts', and crews' families also.

For the next year or so, he kept seven or eight trucks, pulling new factory homes from Mississippi and Alabama to his five sales lots. I drove that road so many times from Lexington, Mississippi to Benton, Missouri from one factory that I believe Brownie could drive himself while I slept. I wish I had kept an exact count on the new homes we pulled for that dealer in Missouri. I believe, in that year and a half, it would be close to 250 or possibly even more.

All those lease drivers and I, along with all the escort drivers, learned to hate and love those trips. We hated the long endless drive to Mississippi: pulling all day and part of the next to Missouri, then driving back home that night, traveling nearly 900 miles on each trip. With our CB radios in every truck, we could talk back and forth to break up the boredom of the pulls. Each driver and each escort driver had what they call a CB handle or nickname to use when talking to each other on those radios.

I had been pegged as Preacher Man, not Boss Man, because I was always preaching to everyone to do a good job. I was raised knowing "if you're gonna do something, do it right." My brother's CB handle was Romeo. As you might guess, he was always trying to sweet talk the ladies, even if it seldom worked, and he really didn't mean anything by it. You remember the Joker, who bribed that scale officer in Louisiana with Christmas spirits? Then, there was GI Joe, respectively named after the army fatigues he wore everywhere he went. One of the others was Miss

Butterscotch, a big, heavy set older woman, and one of the best escort drivers that I ever pulled a mobile home behind. She was all business, and I liked that a lot. She would get in front of Brownie and I and wave that red stick flag in the faces of oncoming cars till they would pull over onto the shoulders of the road, private driveways, and yes, even ditches to let me pass. I always knew when she was flagging in from of me; I never needed to slow down or stop. She'd have the road cleared off before the mobile home and I got there. She was my escort and one of the most professional, finest women I have every met in this business.

My Dad, who had started escorting by then, was called Slowpoke because you couldn't hurry him, and it took him forever to tell you anything in his slow Southern drawl. My niece named herself Luscious Legs. She always wore shorts with socks that matched the color of her clothes, no matter how loud or bright those colors. I still don't know how she managed to find all those colored socks.

We surely had a crew of interesting people. Most of the time, four or five of us would leave the factory about the same time. Of all the talk we had with each other on those radios during these trips, most of it can't be told in public. We worked long tiring hours, but we all had fun and enjoyed working together. And the money wasn't half bad either.

When we all rolled into Missouri with those mobile homes and got unhitched, it was a race to make it to one last stop before we headed home. There's a restaurant in Sikeston, Missouri that is famous for homemade heavy yeast rolls and home cooked meals. You place an order from the menu that includes an entrée and three vegetables. Then, while your order is being prepared, the waitresses come by with pots and bowls of different vegetables, unfold a napkin in from you, and let you test the food. Those homemade yeast rolls are thrown at you from across the restaurant. If you happen to miss one, that's okay, because they will keep on throwing them until you catch a hot one. It's a fun place to eat, and we all loved the good food and atmosphere each time before we headed home.

I don't recall who coined the phrase, "Let the good times roll," but in these first years with Homes, Inc., the good times did allow us to roll a million miles down the highways with those mobile homes.

Chapter Three
Homes Inc.—Bad Times

Up until this point in time, the mobile home business had been very good to me. For someone with only a sixth grade education, I had managed to make a good living not only for myself, but for several families who had joined our Homes, Inc. team. In those two years, we managed to sell 1,085 repos for cash to wholesalers, dealers, and to the public. We had been very fortunate in this business, but the repo market was beginning to slow down. The finance company was getting slower and slower about mailing out checks for work we had done. My dealer in Missouri had five lots full of new and used homes, and only a few per month were selling, leaving us with only a few mobile home pulls each month. My drivers were getting worried about not having enough work, and a couple of them had already gotten nervous and asked us to terminate their lease. We were also getting worried. We remembered how it felt to go without a paycheck when we first started Homes, Inc. It wasn't something we wanted to experience again if there were any possible way to avoid it. Susan and I knew it was time to do something, and we better come up with something before the whole operation fell apart.

Finally, with the passing of time and a little luck on our side, the worst of the recession was ending. New mobile home dealers were beginning to open up sales lots in our area, and we thought this would be the opportunity that we needed to get back on top. I knew I needed to go after some of the work these new dealers might have to offer. So, I decided to put on my best cowboy boots, jeans, and shirt and pay these new dealers a visit. I walked in cold turkey, introduced myself, and then proceeded to present them with the best price I could offer to get the delivery and setup on their new mobile home sales. One lot in particular liked what I had to say and decided to give us a chance. The owner had bought a few repos from us from time to time in the past and had liked our work back then. After doing a few trial runs for him to refresh his memory, he decided to let us pull and setup the homes. Every Friday, he would harass Susan when she presented our bills to him by acting like we were overcharging him. But I will say this—he never cheated us out of one thin dime, and his checks were as good as having money already in the bank.

At one time, during this venture, he decided that the factory was charging too much to pull his new homes from Gulfport, Mississippi to his lot in Arkansas. So we agreed to pick them up, which would save him a little more money. Then he came up with another bright idea to save even more money. He decided that he would put an escort light on his personal pickup, with wide load signs and red flags, so he could run as one of the escorts. By this time, sixteen wide mobile homes were approved for entry into Arkansas, and the law says that you have to run both an escort on the front and rear of the mobile home. But making that first trip with him was one that I'll ever forget. Everyone else had work scheduled and couldn't make that particular trip. Susan agreed to go with us and drive one of the escort trucks. I told him that we would try and leave Alexander, Arkansas for Gulfport, Mississippi that afternoon by 3:00 P.M. I don't remember what business situations held me up that day, but by the time I finished with work, arrived home, ate supper, and showered, it was nearly 8:30 P.M. before we could leave.

Susan and I both knew when we left that if we drove straight to Gulfport, it would be 4:00 A.M. before we arrived, but the dealer apparently hadn't given it any thought. Somewhere around 2:00 A.M., he began getting sleepy and tired. With his CB radio in hand, he let us know he was having a hard time staying awake while driving. Our idea was to pull over for coffee and stretch our legs for a bit, which would keep us all alert for the rest of the drive. I also suggested to Susan that she drive in front of him, so he could follow her red lights because, by now, the fog was heavy around us. One good thing about having Susan along on these late night trips was, no matter what time of the morning and how tired she was, she never faltered in her driving. It was straight as a string. When we finally made it to Gulfport, it was nearly 4:30 A.M....The dealer was tired and worn out and couldn't wait to get his own motel room. I tried to tell him that all we needed was one room because we didn't have much time to sleep. All we had time for was to stretch out and relax for a couple of hours, then shower and get back to work. We had to be at the factory by 7:30 A.M. or we wouldn't get back to Alexander that same day.

Now, when this dealer agreed to escort his mobile home, he had all the wrong ideas in his head. First of all, his pickup was a four-wheel drive Ford with a 440 motor in it, causing him to stop every 200 miles to fuel up. He thought we'd drive down, get a hot meal, and get a nice motel room for the night. Then the next morning, while we hitched to the new mobile home, he would leisurely visit with his factory sales representative. That would have been great, but in Arkansas, we have curfew laws about wide loads. You can't travel on any two-lane highway from 3:00 to 5:00 P.M. because of the school buses being on the road and stopping to let children off. If we didn't leave Gulfport no later than 8:15 A.M., we'd end up sitting somewhere between Lake Village and Pine Bluff on the side of the road, waiting for curfew to end. Reluctantly, without time for breakfast or a casual visit with his sales rep, we rolled away from the factory toward home early the next morning.

Just as we headed north out of Jackson, Mississippi, the dealer, who is a diabetic, started hollering that we needed to look for a restaurant because he wanted a good home cooked meal. I was slowly losing my patience when I answered him, "Do you see a restaurant with great big wide entrances and huge parking spaces to pull this sixteen by eighty mobile home and twenty-four-foot truck into? Have you lost your mind?"

Susan also got on her radio and reminded him that we had to keep going, or we wouldn't get past Pine Bluff to the four-lane highways before curfew.

I finally gave in and said, "We'll stop at the next truck stop and use the restroom, grab a snack, and keep boogying up the road."

I don't believe he said ten words until we got to his sales lot just barely before dark. As I was unhooking Brownie from his mobile home, he came up and said, "Maybe next time I go, it will be different, and we can have an earlier start."

On his last trip with us, somewhere around Grady, Arkansas, a severe thunderstorm with high winds came up, preventing us from traveling any farther. The only thing to do was pull off the road or risk having the mobile home blown off the road. With stormy weather, night came quickly, and we knew we wouldn't make it that day. On the way back home, the dealer made me an offer, "I'll pay you some extra if you will just carry one of your escorts back down there to finish in the morning. I'm officially done. I won't do this again."

He never went with us again and was very happy to pay our price to get his homes pulled and escorted by us. We still remain close friends to this day. Just recently, he bought a few mobile homes from me to setup in his park. But he still complains about what we charge him to move them, and he still writes us a check.

On another trip for this dealer, I took Miss Butterscotch (my favorite escort) and my oldest son, Chris, to drive my escort truck. My son is a good boy, but if he were a game show, it would be called "A Million Questions." He can't help it. He just wants to know when we are leaving, where we are going, whose going with us, when will we be back, and even more, if you get the drift. He can't help himself; it is just his nature. These factory trips don't pay much, and I always tried to save every penny I could to make the most money possible on these trips. When we arrived in Gulfport, we were all starving and needed a good meal, especially at night. When you are fighting fatigue, curfew times, limited daylight hours, and needing to be somewhere else the next day for another job, you had to keep rolling. And stopping for food wasn't always an option. We finally found a restaurant and ate, and then we were ready to find a motel and lay our heads down and rest for the night.

The only motel we found that showed a vacancy looked promising, but when I tried to reserve two rooms, I was told that there was only one room left. Driving until we could find two rooms for a few hours was out of the question. So I did what I thought best and paid for the room. There was nothing else I could do because everyone was exhausted.

After paying for the room and getting the key, we drove around to our room and began getting our bags out. Chris and I grabbed our bag and locked our trucks securely. Miss Butterscotch did the same. It wasn't unusual for Miss Butterscotch and me to stay in one motel room. This was a normal, customary behavior for us; we'd done it a lot of times. We thought nothing of it because these long trips are exhausting, and all you ever wanted to do on these trips was to lay down to get a few hours sleep. You knew that the next day would be another long exhausting trip. Also, reserving one room helped both of us to be able to take more money home when the trip was over. But on this trip, my son, Chris, with a million questions, was with us. I noticed that Chris wasn't saying much when all three of us shut the door on that one room. Miss Butterscotch, seeing an opportunity for a little fun, caught my eye and winked and grinned at me before she said, "Chris, I guess you didn't know I was sleeping with your Dad, did you?"

He looked at both of us with a blank expression and was speechless for once when we both burst out in hysterical laughter. I asked Chris then, "What's wrong, cat got your tongue, son? We are only kidding you. There's only one room, and you will sleep with me. She will sleep in the other bed. It's okay, son, we've done this before. Sometimes we have to do this to save money, and that's all there is to it." We all had a good laugh then.

When we got home, I told Susan this story. Knowing how naive Chris was, she said she could just imagine what went through his head when we told him that. She laughed and told Miss Butterscotch and I that we should be ashamed of ourselves for pulling that on him.

But on another trip to the factory, Miss Butterscotch couldn't make it, so another lady escort volunteered to work with me. This trip was a fourteen-wide mobile home, and I only needed to have one escort on this trip. When the day ended, we arrived at the same motel as before, and again, they only had one room available with a single bed. I had never stayed in the same motel room with this woman before, but it was all strictly part of the business. I never imagined her reaction. At first, she didn't say anything, but when I unlocked the door and she saw that it had a single, solitary bed, she looked at me with hands on her hips and said, "I'm not staying in here and sleeping with you!"

I looked at her and said, "Suit yourself, but this is the only room we can get. I'm taking a shower and lying down to sleep. I promise to sleep on my side with my back to you, and I suggest that if you want any sleep, you do the same. You can sleep in your jeans if that will make you feel better."

Well, she went in the bathroom and stayed for a good long while. When she came out, she had freshened her makeup, brushed her hair, and got all prettied up in a hot pink nightie. She looked over at me and said, "I don't sleep with any man unless he helps pay my bills."

I couldn't help it. I was tired and nearly half asleep when I popped off my mouth, "Honey, I can barely pay my own bills. I don't want you, and I love Susan very much. I'm going to sleep. I suggest you do the same."

She then jerked her pillow off the bed, threw it on the floor, and, as far as I know, slept there all night. I was still chuckling under my breath when I went to sleep. She escorted with me a lot more times after that, but we never had to stay in the same room again.

We also started working for a new mobile home dealer across the interstate. Now, working for a new mobile home dealer is different than all those repos we had gotten used to. Now, when you are dealing with the public buying a brand new *home*, most of the time, they want everything in their brand new home to be perfect. The dealer has to make the customer happy, and we have to make the dealer happy with the work we do, as well as the new homeowner. We quickly learned to adapt to this new type of work. If the customer wanted the white refrigerator out (for free), we removed it and put the black refrigerator that they requested in (for free), took the blue couch out (for free) and put the brown couch in (for free). A lot of you are probably thinking, "That's not much to ask, since it's their money." But they ask it just as you are ready to roll off the sales lot with that new home. I have just called the customer to meet me in one hour about fifty miles away. But we just grin, bear it, and adapt to the situation, because I will learn that all new mobile home dealers expect these same courtesies.

This particular dealer was selling a lot of new homes, and they were keeping us busy. Most of the homes were double-wides, and there is a lot of work connecting those two halves together. It requires two trucks, two escorts, two helpers, and a lot of setup materials that we have to pay for out of our pocket, such as concrete blocks, treated wood plates and wedges, and steel anchors to secure them to the ground. The average bill to that dealer on a double-wide would be about 3,000 dollars. We were delivering two or three per week for them at this time.

Our arrangement was to collect payment each Friday for what homes we had delivered. It worked just that way for quite a long time, but things started to change. Susan would go each Friday to pick up our check, so we could pay our payroll, our fuel bill, and our suppliers for setup materials. Soon, the dealer began to tell us that his money was "a little tight this week," so they asked if it would be all right if they pay us the following week when they fund their customer's loans? They paid us a lot of money, so we tried to be patient and understand their situation. We had been tight on money before also. But eventually, it evolved into every two weeks when they pay. Before long, they were almost thirty days behind paying us. I finally had no choice but to tell Susan to let them know that today was the last home I would deliver for them until we got paid for the work we had done. These new homes created a lot more expense to Homes, Inc. than the repos. Our labor cost was more than double, and we had all those setup materials to pay for. Our suppliers had to be paid, and we had always paid on time, but we were running out of money. I delivered that home, and Susan and I made up our minds to go up there the next morning and demand our money. Unfortunately, we had, for the first time in our business, trusted the wrong people. We were told by the manager that they had filed bankruptcy the week before. They owed us over 42,000 dollars, but the manager said we would get our money through the courts over time. We soon got bankruptcy papers in the mail. We filled them out and filed them with the court. We soon learned that their debt was so great we might not get any money. They shut their doors up tight, and we never received a penny of that money to this day.

At about this same time, a dealer from southern Missouri came down and agreed to buy seventeen repos wholesale from us. He paid for the homes and told us that he would pay us for the delivery when we got the homes to his lot. It was tough now because we had already lost 42,000 dollars. Payroll taxes were due in a couple of weeks, and we had to pay all our suppliers, even though we hadn't collected one penny of that money. We had to terminate more lease drivers because the plentiful work was no longer there. We couldn't pay them when we didn't collect. We just knew that, when we got those repos to southern Missouri, everything would be okay again. We finished the job as we agreed, and he wrote us a check. Susan deposited that check the next day in the bank, and then signed our tax form for the payroll taxes and dropped a check for them in the mail to the IRS. Maybe we would be okay again. Well, guess what? His check to us bounced. He promised that it was a bank mistake and told us to just deposit it again, and we did. But it bounced again. Susan reminded me of what was about to happen. "That check to the IRS is going to bounce any day, and then we will be in big trouble."

A week later, that check bounced. We had already started scrambling for work to get money in the bank before the IRS swooped down on us. But things were taking a turn for the worst at Homes, Inc., and it was coming from every direction.

At that time in the State of Arkansas, due to a crazy law enacted back in 1950, only three mobile home transporters had the right to pull mobile homes intrastate. Intrastate meant picking a mobile home up from some point in Arkansas and delivering it to another point in Arkansas without crossing a state line. For about a year now, Homes, Inc. (trying to keep our head above water) had been going around that law a little bit. We didn't do it to be dishonest, we just wanted to continue to work and make a living. We did not have intrastate authority. So, when we would move a mobile home from Alexander to Benton, we would call our oversize permit in from the Tennessee state line to Benton, Arkansas. Since we had interstate authority, we thought no one will be the wiser. We had been doing this a lot in order to work for those dealers in my home state of Arkansas.

One morning, Susan received a registered letter in the mail from the Arkansas Highway Transportation Commission regarding complaints from one of the other transporters, who did have intrastate authority, stating that they had filed a formal complaint with this commission against Homes, Inc. They had found twenty illegal permits obtained by Homes, Inc. and were going to fine us 1,000 dollars per permit. She looked at me and said, "What the hell are we going to do now?" Not only were we facing a huge fine, but if we got another permit illegally and falsified our route, we could serve prison time!

After some thought, I knew I had only one slim chance to resolve this. That mobile home tycoon in Conway had told me that if I ever needed a favor, just call. I knew he had a lot of political pull in the mobile home industry in Arkansas, and it was time to make that call to see if he could or would try to help us. I faxed him the letter the commission had sent me, and I argued that it just didn't seem right, considering that I was born, raised, and had lived in this state all my life and could be denied the right to work in my own state. He knew about the law and said it was crazy, but nobody had ever challenged that 1950 law. Everyone who pulled mobile homes intrastate in Arkansas had always been leased to one of those three transport companies until we formed Homes, Inc. He said to me, "Bobby, I'm sorry, but you have been stepping on the wrong toes for a while, and you just stepped on one toe too many. I've been friends with the owners of that transport company who filed those complaints. I don't know what I can do, but I will try to help you."

I thanked him and wondered—when we hung up our phones—if he really meant that or was he just brushing me off. The next afternoon, he called the office and told me I would be getting a letter in the mail from the Arkansas Highway Transportation Commission, dismissing all the fines and charges. But the condition of this dismissal was that Homes, Inc. would no longer pull another mobile home intrastate in Arkansas ever again. It was the biggest favor anyone in this business has ever given me to this day. Thank God he was my friend. He had bailed me out of this jam, and my favor had been repaid as promised.

But Susan and I knew, in that moment, that Homes, Inc. was done. We had very little work moving mobile homes out of state, and we still owed the IRS 27,000 dollars plus interest and penalties for that bounced check. We had no money to pay it. We called all our partners in and told them the news. Someone told us to hire a tax attorney, and they would be able to get those taxes reduced or dismissed if we filed bankruptcy on the company. We paid that attorney 1,000 dollars only to find out that you cannot be released from employee payroll taxes even with a bankruptcy. We would have to pay those taxes.

We're done, we had no choice but to bankrupt Homes, Inc. and shut down the business. If we wanted to stay in the mobile home business, each of us could take a toter truck and lease it to our competitor, so we could work or find jobs. None of us knew what the IRS would eventually do about not paying those taxes, but we had to support our families, and the IRS was shoved into the back of our minds for now.

Chapter Four
Working for the Competition

Well, now, I'm the president of a bankrupted company without a job. My partners and all the crew and their families who depended on me are in the same boat. I realize I've got to do something quick before this boat begins to sink. I swallowed all the pride in me that I could muster and drove to one of my competitors' office to talk to them about leasing my truck. I could not bring myself to talk with the competitor who had filed a complaint on Homes Inc. and nearly cost me thousands of dollars in fines. Some of the drivers who had been leased to me suggested that I talk to the terminal agent at Transit Homes of America, Inc. The terminal agent of this company was receptive to me, but she was very aware of the closing of Homes, Inc. and asked me about our other three trucks. I told her that I couldn't be positive of what my partners were going to do yet, but I felt sure we would all four want to lease in to Transit Homes of America, Inc., if they would have us.

She outlined the lease papers with me and summarized the pay schedule. When you work for a big company like them, they take a percentage from your check with each freight bill you submit. Each check would have 25 percent of the freight withheld and 35 percent of your labor withheld. Now, I understood them taking part of my freight to pay their bills. But to give them 35 percent of the backbreaking labor I did was a lot of bull to me. I held my cool, all the time reaching for those papers to fill out for my lease agreement with this company. Reluctantly, I went home to give Susan the news.

My other partners were anxious to hear about this meeting and were waiting to see how it went. We all sat down and decided that each partner, except our silent partner, would take one of the toter trucks for themselves and keep the drivers who had been driving them. Susan and I had made our decision. There seemed to be no other choice at the moment for us. After all, with my child support to my ex-wife for my three boys and Susan's son and three daughters, I had to start bringing a paycheck home fast to support our large family.

This company was licensed to transport nationwide, and there was a lot for me to get done before my lease agreement with them could be activated. I had to pass a drug test and get my DOT physical card. My truck had to have a DOT inspection. Homes, Inc. decals had to be removed from the doors of my truck so new Transit Homes of America, Inc. decals could be added. A report of my driving record had to be sent from the State of Arkansas and a criminal background check was done. In three days, I hustled around and managed to get everything I needed, and my lease was activated. I was officially one of about 500 drivers leased to this company nationwide. They had terminal locations in nearly every state, and I could work for any of them that needed me. I sure hoped some of them needed me soon!

Now, when you're the new driver, you're at the bottom of the totem pole when calls come in for homes to be moved. Everyone was watching me like the new kid on the block. At first, my new terminal agent seemed like she didn't like me. She would give me the calls that paid very little, and when I would protest, she said, "That's all I got. Take it or go back home." The other drivers were resentful of another driver because the work wasn't really plentiful right now anyway. I accepted any and everything the terminal agent gave me to do. I remembered again how I had tried so hard at farming, assembly line work, and my own company. I knew somehow that I could make this work and be successful with this, too, if I tried my hardest.

My first big break came one morning when another driver refused to go and deliver a new mobile home for a dealer in Jacksonville. For some reason, they had a disagreement, and she called my terminal agent and asked her to send someone else to deliver her mobile home that day. My agent called me in and said, "Bobby, this lady that owns this mobile home dealership is really hard to work for. She gives us a lot of work, and Roy has been delivering and installing all her new homes. Do you think you can handle this for me today?"

I looked at her and said, "Haven't I done everything so far you asked me without a hitch? I'll sure give it a whirl."

When I drove up to that lot in Jacksonville and went in to their office, I met one of the foxiest young business women I will ever be associated with. She was blunt and to the point with me. "I sell a lot of new mobile homes, and I want my job done right. I'm tired of Roy's crap. He is not courteous to my customers and half ass sets up my homes. Do you think you can do a good job?"

I looked at her across that desk and told her, "You betcha! Give me directions to the customer's site and show me which home to deliver."

We shook hands, and off I went to start my beginning of what would be a huge account in the near future.

The next day, my terminal manager called me into her office. She told me that the dealer's customer had called the dealer and complimented me on the good job and how courteous I had been. The lady at that dealership had requested that I deliver more homes for her in the near future. I breathed a huge sigh of relief that maybe now, things would get better again. You'll hear later how this first dealer and our relationship grew into something really great for myself and all my prior partners.

One morning, I was sitting at the terminal with several other drivers waiting to see if there was any work. On this particular morning, my regional manager for the company was in the office with my terminal agent. She brought him out and introduced me as a new driver in the fleet. He was cordial enough, but soon turned from me to address an issue with three of my fellow drivers sitting around joking and drinking coffee. He turned to each of them and asked, "What are y'all doing sitting around here? I gave you fifteen loads for those repossessed mobile homes a week ago from Texas to here in Jacksonville. I just got my butt chewed out by our customer. He said not one home had been picked up or delivered yet."

Each one of those drivers gave him some different lame excuse on why they hadn't done any of them yet, and he stormed back to my agent's office and slammed the door shut.

Now, I had just met this man a few minutes before this happened. I didn't know what would happen to me after I boldly walked down the hall and knocked on that door. I could already feel heat steaming out around those hinges on my terminal agent's door. But I've never been bashful when it comes to work and making a dollar. I hesitated a few seconds before raising my hand to knock and stepped in the office. I looked at my regional manager and big as life blurted out, "Boss, my partners and I leased four trucks to this terminal, and we'll go get those homes for you starting tomorrow. I think we can get all of them by the end of next week if you'll give them to us."

He looked at me puzzled and then looked over at my terminal agent and asked, "Is this boy a good driver? If we don't do something quick, we'll lose these loads to Brand X (as we all called the other competitor)!"

She told him, "Bobby has done everything I have asked him to do as agreed. Give him the loads because those other boys sure haven't been interested in doing the job apparently."

My prior partners and I pulled all fifteen of those repos from Texas in five days. Brownie and I had sure enough made "brownie points" with my regional manager, and it would soon pay off in a big way.

Not long after that, one of the regional manager's favorite drivers had taken a home for some folks to Alabama and wrecked it up pretty bad. The driver and the regional manager had already been in several heated discussions about that home and the way he had handled the problem with our company's customer. The driver was in the office, complaining about not getting any long, big paying loads. The regional manager told him that until he learned to be more responsible, he wouldn't get them either. He said the insurance claim on that last damaged home was huge

My Home Has Wheels—Please Move Me

and still not settled yet. Before this driver had a chance to storm out of the terminal, my agent walked out with a good load from down in Mississippi back to Arkansas. The regional manager turned to my agent and pointed to me and said, "Give this one to Bobby. He deserves a good load."

I knew at that moment that I was really "in like Flynn" now.

I remember one time when my brother and I took a load to move a double-wide mobile home from Georgia to Tennessee. We drove half the night to get there and worked nearly all day the next day to separate both halves, get the shipping plastic nailed on each side, and try to pull it a ways before dark caught us. As luck would have it, we got to a set of Georgia scales just before dark, and they pulled us in and told us to shut it down for the night. As we were locking our trucks and getting in the escort trucks to find a motel for the night, the DOT officer at the scales came walking out to the back of our trucks. He said, "Well, have you boys from Arkansas ever pulled a mobile home in Georgia before?"

I looked at him and said, "No, sir, this is our first time."

He said, "Well, I guess you boys may be here awhile. You don't have your company sign on the back of your homes, and I might have to detain you and let Georgia keep some of that Arkansas money!"

I was bone tired from working all day, but I knew you don't question the DOT. My brother asked, "We're out in the middle of nowhere. How the hell are we going to get a sign with the company name, address, and phone number on it by morning?"

I didn't know the answer to his question, but my dad always told me, "Where there's a will, there's a way." I had to find that way. I woke up that next morning still not knowing where to get that sign made.

As I was brushing my teeth and combing my hair, I got a brainstorm. I told my brother, "Jump in the truck and find a service station, and bring me back a big black magic marker."

He said, "You know, poster board won't work. It will be in shreds before we get down the road a mile?"

I knew that, but that wasn't what I had in mind. He left and brought back a marker in short order. I had stripped two white pillowcases off the pillows on our bed and had them stretched flat on the floor. I took that marker and printed our company name, address, and phone number on those white pillowcases. We drove up to the scales and quickly attached those pillowcases firmly to the back of each half of the home. When the DOT officer pulled up and walked back to us, he scratched his head and started laughing, and said, "Well, boys, that's a first for me, but the regulations don't say what that sign must be made of. I guess you better get out of my scale house before I find something to fine you boys for."

We got the hell out of Georgia!

One of our terminal agents out of Jackson, Mississippi gave my brother and I a double-wide office building to take from Jackson to South Carolina. The second day on the road, we were pulling up and down a rolling, hilly two-lane road in north Alabama. A flock of wild turkeys flew out of the woods into the road, and one of them smashed into the front of my brother's office building. We looked for a wide spot and pulled off the road to check the damage. Pulling down the road at about fifty-five miles an hour, it had smashed and dented three sheets of metal on the front of his building. We tried to straighten the metal and nailed it down as best we could. When we arrived the next day at our destination, the lady in charge came out to do her walk around and sign our paperwork so we could get our pay. When she got to my brother's building and looked up to see the smashed metal, she asked, "What happened to my office building?"

I told you my brother's CB handle was Romeo. This was just one reason why. He replied, "Ma'am, this huge wild turkey came out of the woods from nowhere and flew smack dab into the front of my building. I didn't know at first what hit me," and then he grinned really big.

She looked at him without hesitation and jokingly replied, "Yeah, 'Wild Turkey,' how much of it did you drink?" Then, she laughed really hard and asked for his paperwork to sign and wrote "NO DRIVER DAMAGES" on it. She told him to forget about it and have a safe trip home. She'd take care of that smashed metal. Romeo did have a way with those women.

Another terminal agent in south Mississippi gave me a trip for a military guy moving from Biloxi, Mississippi to Los Angeles, California. She told me that it was a twelve-by-sixty mobile home, and I wouldn't need an escort. Now, that's a long way to haul a mobile home, and my unloaded miles were way more than my loaded miles. When she told me that this trip paid over 10,000 dollars, I was headed for Mississippi. I guess this was when I realized that I like these long hauls. Now then, our government really took care of our boys in the service. They were paying me to pack this man's personal belongings, unblock it, put tires on it, and pull the anchors up out of the ground. It was going to a mobile home park in L.A., and I had to unpack it, re-block it, and put the anchors back in the ground. I figured I could make this trip in about a week, and then back home. When I arrived in Biloxi, I was disheartened, though. My twelve-by-sixty mobile home was an eight-by-thirty-six travel trailer. All the personal belongings had already been removed, and it was sitting on four new tires. I called the agent and told her of the circumstances.

She replied, "Bobby, that's your good fortune. All our paperwork has been signed and pay was authorized for the whole deal. You'll get paid the same regardless." Hooray for me!

I had heard horror stories from drivers about those scales houses at the California line. All the drivers at my terminal warned me that they hated mobile home toter trucks out there. Only few of them had been brave enough to venture out there. In California, you drive into a huge building on ramps, with a pit underneath, and those DOT officers go over your truck from underneath and above ground. I was scared to death with this picture planted in my brain. But you have to understand that Brownie was my livelihood, and I prided myself in keeping him in top notch shape mechanically; it was also always clean and neat. When Brownie and I got the green light to roll off those scales and ramps, I knew my trip would be a success.

I had one more obstacle though upon arriving in L.A. There had been a mistake made at the mobile home park. They had no lots vacant to put my travel trailer. I called the agent in Mississippi, and she made arrangements for me to store my travel trailer at a facility in L.A. and to come home. Now, this was during all the Rodney King riots in L.A., and this storage facility was in one of those worst parts of the city. When I got there, the guard asked me if I was crazy driving through that bad neighborhood with my trailer. He gave me a safer route out of there and all I had on my mind was Arkansas now.

I drove straight through from L.A., and by the time I got near Oklahoma City, it had started snowing really hard. The roads were becoming hazardous, and Brownie and I were starting to slide all over the place. I slid down an off ramp and made it to a truck stop. I had been driving way too long. I went into the restaurant, ordered a cheeseburger and coke, then called Susan and told her that I would eat and start on home. Then I woke up. The waitress had rolled up my jacket and laid my head on it and pulled off my boots from my swollen feet. She was coming toward me with the food and drink that I had ordered five hours before. She said, "Man, I don't know where you came from, but you looked like a zombie. When you fell asleep, I couldn't help but try and make you more comfortable. I knew when you got still, you weren't going any farther."

There are a lot of really good people out there in this big world. I guess this trip is the one I pushed a little too hard on to make a dollar!

Now, being on top of the list for these big, good paying trips was great for me, but it was causing a lot of resentment with the other drivers. I never understood it 'cause a lot of times, they were offered the trips before me and refused to go and do them. But I got the cold shoulder from them a lot. I didn't have time for their whining and complaining. All I had in my mind was getting on top again.

An agent in Florida talked to the terminal agent in south Mississippi, and she told her that I would take the long trips and do her a good job. She called and asked me to move a lady from Florida to St. Louis, Missouri. She was very thorough about the details on her trips. She explained to me that the customer who owned this fourteen-by-seventy mobile home was mentally challenged, and all my dealings would have to be with the woman's sister who was paying for the trip. The agent had half of my money up front, but I would have to collect the balance in St. Louis from the sister upon delivery. When we got to the truck stop near where our mobile home was, the girl at the fuel desk told us that this park was in a nearly all-Cuban neighborhood. She said if you go down there, they might strip your trucks, steal your tools, or even kill you. It was a very dangerous area, and I had better call the city police to take us in there. I called the city and an officer took us there. But then he told me he was leaving, and I was on my own. The lady met us at her door and proceeded to cuss me out 'cause the moving van had not arrived yet. I called the moving company for her, and they asked what size of van they were supposed to bring. She was hollering and cussing in my cell phone (her phone had been disconnected) to bring the biggest truck they had, and they had better hurry up. She told them that her sister had already given them a credit card for the truck, and they were holding me up. Within thirty minutes, an older black man and two helpers rolled up in an eighteen-wheeler Atlas Van Lines Truck, pulling a fifty-two-foot van box. He jumped out and asked if he was at the right place, and I pointed over to the lady we were moving. He told me, "It won't take me and these boys long to pack and load her home. Then you can be on your way."

I laughed and told him, "No, it won't take long at all. All she has left in the mobile home is a recliner. And she wants you to haul that metal yard swing and push lawnmower."

He looked at me and said, "Man, are you pulling my leg, is this a joke?"

I told him "no," and he insisted on calling his terminal to verify it. He tried to explain, but his terminal told him to load up her things. They had the sister's credit card. He would get paid in full to haul her belongings. With that, the old black man started singing, "Thank you, Jesus, I love you, Jesus."

He told his two helpers to load the three items, and I heard a few last words as he climbed into that big moving truck. "Jesus does take care of an old man who tries hard. Thank you, Jesus."

All this time, Cubans were filling the streets around us. He could tell I was getting nervous, and he looked at me and said,

"Just get behind and follow me out of here, boy. They won't bother you. They'll move over out of your way." And they did.

When I got to St. Louis, I asked for the other half of my money. It was our company's strict policy to collect our balance and any other incurred expenses before unhooking a truck from a mobile home. The lady didn't have any money, and, at first, I couldn't reach her sister. I called Susan, and she told me to sit tight. She would call the home office and ask what to do. The man in charge of claims in Boise asked if they had a credit card. I finally told the lady that if her sister didn't appear soon, I was going to take her home to a storage facility and unhook from it. About one hour later, her sister drove up in a big new Lincoln with diamonds on every finger. She asked what the problem was. I told her I wanted the rest of my money before I unhook the truck and finished the move. She handed me an American Express card and told me there's no problem. I called Boise back and gave him the credit card information. I told him, "Look, with all my flat tires on this trip, waiting time arguing with this customer, and new blocks I had to buy, the balance she owed is 8,300 dollars."

He ran the card and came back to me in a couple of minutes. He said, "Bobby, we have all 13,000 dollars of your money on this trip. Get her to sign your paperwork and finish her home." This was my first experience with having to call the home office with a problem like this, and I was sure glad someone was home.

Now, I had been to Disney World before with my boys once, and, as an adult, I was not impressed. But this next trip was a little more impressive. My son, Chris, and I went to move a mobile home for a young couple in Louisiana to Florida. This home was sitting vacant for some time in a grown-up, murky swamp in south Louisiana. I knew that Brownie was too heavy to bog out in that mud to the mobile home. I called the customer and told them that the only way to get their home was to hire a bulldozer and keep its tracks and the wheels of my truck on sheets of plywood, so it wouldn't sink. She said, "I need my home and will pay you whatever it takes to get it here, no matter what the cost."

My son and I found a bulldozer and used twenty-four sheets of triple stacked plywood to keep that home, the bulldozer, and Brownie from sinking in the murky mess. It took us two whole days to get that mobile home out of the mud. When we got to the Florida scales, we were overweight by nearly 800 pounds, and the scale officer was threatening to fine us. I thought a minute and asked him, "Sir, don't you need a couple of hundred concrete blocks at your house? If I unload them out of my toter truck and stack them up really neat behind these scales, couldn't you take them home and use them somehow?" Believe me or not, this really worked, and he let us unload those blocks and leave without a fine. Sometimes, you just have to be a little creative to make these jobs work.

As I get really close to my location in Florida, I called my customer again to get directions from her. She told me to turn on Highway 4 and take the first road to the right. I asked her to repeat those directions because I had been seeing signs about Disney World pointing that way. But she was insistent on her directions. I gave my son those directions and there we went. I hadn't gone far when I realized that I was driving up to the front entrance and gate of Disney World.

I am pulling a mobile home with mud on the tires, metal covered with thick, green moss up to the Epcot Center of Disney World with no way to back up or turn this mobile home around. I told my son, "Hurry up and make this loop back out of here. We're at Disney World!"

He said, "I know, Dad. There's Mickey Mouse waving hello to us."

People were pointing, stating, and laughing. I think they thought we were part of a new act for Disney World. I just wanted to make the loop and get out of there before someone called the law. About then, a security guard flagged us down to stop, and I thought we are in trouble now. But he just laughed and said," Are you boys having a little problem?"

I explained about the wrong directions, and he told me that we should have made a left turn instead of turning right. He helped direct us back out of the Disney World property, and I called the customer again to meet us. How would you like to visit Disney World this way?

In January, I had been with the company for about eight months. Things were going great, and I was making really good money again. Brownie and I pulled up to the terminal, and I noticed a bunch of the drivers' trucks and the regional manager's car out front. When I walked in, I was told to take a seat. The regional manager had an important announcement to make. I had no idea what was about to happen. The regional manager looked around the room to everyone, and then his eyes stopped on me when he announced, "Well, everyone, I have been asked by the home office in Boise, Idaho to make an announcement this morning. Every year, our company awards one driver, in our fleet of 500 drivers, an award for Driver of the Year. This year, the winner of this award is Bobby Henley from our terminal."

I stared at him in amazement as all eyes turned to me. That couldn't be true. There must be a mistake. I had only been leased in for eight months, and we had 500 drivers nationwide. But it was true. Brownie and I had produced more revenue, without any claims, nationwide than any of those other drivers all year last year.

The next morning, the president of the company called me and said, "Bobby, congratulations on making Driver of the Year for our company. You've done a great job! You'll receive a company embossed jacket and briefcase, a nice plaque with your name on it, and a check for 500 dollars. Also, we want you and your wife to come out to Boise, Idaho to the main office for three days, all expenses paid, to receive your award. My wife and I want to meet you, and you can meet the staff there that keeps this company running smoothly for you drivers. I'll book your flight and let you know when to come."

Flight! He meant get on an airplane to Idaho. This old country boy had crashed twice in those small crop duster planes while working for farmers and walked away both times with only bumps and bruises. I told my Good Lord then that I would never fly again. If he had wanted me to fly, I know he would have given me wings and put feathers on my butt. No, I wasn't going to fly to Idaho for all the awards or money in the world. When I told that to the president of the company, he couldn't believe it. He called Susan, and she tried to convince me that we really needed to go and accept this award. But when I flat-footedly refused, it was decided that the president and his wife would fly here for our annual company picnic later next month and present the awards in person. I got the Driver of the Year for two more years in a row with the company. It became a joke between the president of the company and me. He would call and congratulate me each time, and then he would say, "Bobby, I'll send your awards and check to the terminal again this year."

Chapter Five
United States "Infernal" Revenue Service

When you are a driver of the year for three years running with a major transport company, and your wife really knows her business in the mobile home industry, certain doors and opportunities open up for you. Up to this point, Susan and I were basically running our business from our home. Susan was always a stickler for the paperwork being correct and made sure that all my freight bills, log sheets, and money collected for the company were perfect when I took them to the terminal to submit for my pay. She and I both knew that without the paperwork being correct, the company wouldn't pay us on time.

One morning, Susan went to the terminal to turn in to my agent a stack of paperwork, and she found our terminal agent frustrated and ready to pull her hair out. Drivers weren't where they were supposed to be, permits for loads hadn't been sent on time, other drivers were turning in paperwork for pay, and the phones were ringing off the wall. She looked at Susan all frazzled and said, "I'm going crazy, and I need help here. The home office has told me to hire someone to assist me in this office. Do you need a job?"

Susan looked at her and laughed, "Not really. I have my hands full just keeping up with Bobby and my other truck leased in here. Not to mention all the kids."

But she was dead serious. We had both noticed for some time that the terminal agent was overwhelmed a lot with her workload. Susan mentioned it to me when I got home that night. I told her that she should consider it. It might be to our advantage for her to work there and help with the office. Maybe we would get first shot at some of the better loads that way. And besides, she was already familiar with all the paperwork and how to quote those loads and order permits for the loads. I knew that her pay for this job probably wouldn't be much, but it might increase my pay tremendously, if it worked out. Susan decided to take the position and give it a try.

We opened a checking account when we leased to Transit Homes of America, Inc., with advice from our accountant to keep business income and expenses separate from personal bills. We named our small company B&S Mobile Home Service, after Bobby and Susan. We had our own phone number listed that way also. One of the conditions of Susan being hired as assistant terminal agent was for her to have her own office and for our phone line to be installed in her office, too. The company agreed, as long as it didn't conflict with their business. Most of our work now came from customers who had used me to move mobile homes for them and called me on this B&S line. Seldom did they call my terminal agent to find me.

A call came in one day from a mobile home transport broker out of Texas. He was looking for drivers to do long moves for individuals being transferred by the military, Walmart, and other big companies. He talked with my terminal agent and explained how he worked things, but she told him that she didn't think Transit Homes of America, Inc. would be interested in getting a move through a third party. She respectfully explained that there would be too much liability involved, and she didn't have many drivers interested in moving a mobile home through several states anymore. She told him that most of her drivers didn't want to pull a mobile home out of Arkansas. She thanked him for calling and hung up. Susan had heard this whole conversation and couldn't believe the agent was declining work. She asked our terminal agent if she could have his name and number and visit with him again.

She responded, "I don't care. Call him back if you want, but don't get the company involved. You know, Bobby is the only one that will go out of state any more. If you work out something, y'all are on your own with this man."

Susan called him back and everything they discussed sounded on the up and up. He had been using another transporter to haul a lot of homes, but they had not been doing a very good job. He had brokered these trips for huge amounts of money. He would book the trips and take care of collecting the money for them. When he gave us a trip, he would fax us the details of everything, along with a comcheck number for one half of the total trip. Upon completion of the trip and a call from his customer that the job was done to their satisfaction, he would give us a comcheck number for the balance in full. A comcheck is a blank check you can get at nearly any truck stop. The check can be made out to you, and when a code number is inserted at the top by the sender, it's as good as cash in your hand. He would always guarantee us our money if we would do the work and make the customers happy. Susan and I talked about this. It sounded easy enough, and we decided to try it once. If it didn't work for us, we didn't have to do any more work for him.

Our first trip for the broker was from a town near Niagara Falls, New York to El Paso, Texas. The mobile home was twenty-six miles on top of a mountain. The only thing on top of this mountain was a small town with a mobile home park. To get to the top of this mountain, you have to wind round and round like wrapping a garland around the branches of a Christmas tree. The outside lane of this winding road has only guard rails to keep cars from going off the edge. The closer you got to the top, the smaller the cars below looked, eventually looking like matchbox cars from our viewpoint. My escort on this trip was my cousin whose CB handle was "the Mule." I won't even begin to tell you why that was his handle, so don't ask! Well, Mule was amazed going that twenty-six miles round and round to reach the top of that mountain, and he didn't talk much on his CB radio either. We found the customer and his mobile home and got it ready to roll. He was very cordial, and the last thing we did after shaking hands and he announced we'd see him in Texas, was to sit our half full cup of coffee on the bar and lock the door to his home. Mule was screwing down our wide load signs on the escort truck and hanging his red flags. I knew that he was entirely too quiet for some reason. He looked at me and said, "There is no way I'm going to get in front of you and Brownie going down that mountain pulling a mobile home. Your brakes will never hold on that steep incline."

I could tell he was genuinely scared, but I told him, "Mule, you have no choice. I've got to have an escort down to the bottom. You saw those guard rails, and I won't risk meeting a car and scraping this man's home on those rails."

He was stubborn as a "mule" and flat-footedly refused to go down first that I couldn't get him to budge. But, in the end, I finally relented and decided to go down that mountain first with him dragging up the rear of my home. Somehow, Brownie and I made it to the bottom without an incident, but we were damn lucky we did without an escort truck in front to warn people of us approaching.

Brownie and I pulled that mobile home for over 2,900 miles. When we arrived, our customer met us and was pleased we had made it safely. He unlocked the front door and jumped inside to inspect his home and belongings. With his signature and a phone call to the broker in Texas, I could collect my money for the trip at the first truck stop. I was with him for his inspection and everything looked just the way he had packed it in Niagara Falls, New York. By everything, even the two glass coffee cups, half full of old coffee, had sat untouched in the same spot on that bar without a drop spilled. I become a true believer that day that mobile homes were really mobile even on 2,900 miles of not so smooth highways from near Canada to near Mexico.

I called Susan and told her that I was headed home. She said, "Not so fast. We need to talk before you do. Do you have your comcheck number for our money yet?"

I told her, "I sure do."

She said, "Well, here's the deal. The broker has a mobile home over in Albuquerque, New Mexico to pick up and bring back to Tulsa, Oklahoma. If you can drive over there to get it tomorrow, we'll get paid for you to drive nearly all the way back home."

My head started spinning. I was only about five hours from Albuquerque, and I was twelve hours back to home. I wasn't used to getting paid both directions on a trip. She knew me well, because when I told her, "You bet," she started laughing and said, "I have the information, have ordered your permits, and he gave me your comcheck number for this trip already."

That's when I said, "I guess I'll see you in a couple of days then."

Not all of our customers were happy when we delivered their home to its new destination. I moved a man, retiring from the military, and his wife from Indianapolis, Indiana to West Texas. When we all left, it was agreed that I would call him, and we would meet near Houston so he could lead us to his property. He told us it was a little hard to give directions to it. True to his word, I called him near Houston, and he got out in front of us. I asked him where we were going, He replied, "Lonesome Dove, Texas, where they made the movie."

I told him, "No kidding. I had no idea it was really a town."

We drove and drove, finally turning off a dirt road, then driving almost thirty-six more miles. All I saw was wide, open dry, desolate land, with a few cactus and mesquite bushes scattered about. He motioned for me to stop and pointed where to put his home. At about this same time, his wife got out of the car, sobbing and crying.

She told my escort, "Go get my bags and put them in your escort truck. There is no way I'm staying out here in this God-forsaken place. Had he told me it would look like this, and I'd be isolated from the world, I would have never agreed to come here."

She was really serious, and they began to argue a little. All that time, I'm setting up their mobile home. She pleaded with my escort again, "I'll ride back to Little Rock with you and catch a plane back home. Get my bags."

As we drove away, I could still hear her telling her husband that she wasn't going to stay there. I always wondered whether he talked her into it because I never got a call to move their home somewhere else.

Back then, the phone company didn't have any plans that offered unlimited long distance rates. You paid for every minute of long distance that you talked. The broker from Texas suggested we get a 1-800 number to keep our phone expenses down. He said, "A lot of customers wouldn't call you back if it cost them money to talk to you."

I was gone out of town a lot on these trips. I got lonesome and talked to Susan a lot. We ordered the number and had it installed on Susan's desk. Overall, it saved us money and made us money. You all know I'm all about making money!

For those of you who live out West in those mountain states from Colorado, Utah, Idaho, and Wyoming, you know what your winters are like. You will appreciate this next trip I took for the broker. It was a fourteen-by-seventy mobile home from Biloxi, Mississippi to Idaho Falls, Idaho. That wasn't many more miles than the Niagara Falls trip, but there was just one small snag. It was in January! Susan ordered my permits, and I took off. It was smooth sailing until I got to West Oklahoma. My air bags busted on Brownie, and I had to get it repaired at a truck stop. Those truck stop mechanics are not cheap. Susan wired me some money to pay for the repairs because I only took enough money on each of these trips to make the trip. I got rolling again, but at Denver it started snowing, and I had never seen so much snow. My permits were routed across one of the mountain passes, and it was shut down for heavy snow. I called Susan and told her to find me another route out of Colorado and get me new permits.

When she pulled out her atlas and called me back, she said, "I'm checking the atlas, but I can't find another route west. There are only two major highways on the map—the one going east and west on your permit, and the one going north to Wyoming. That's it for major highways, and I know you don't want me to route you on any two-lane roads. Do you want to try the one north to Cheyenne, Wyoming?"

I told her I sure didn't want to just sit in Denver forever. She ordered and faxed the permits. As I rolled into Cheyenne, the signs at the scales said, "HIGH WIND WARNING IN EFFECT." I didn't know what the hell that meant, but it couldn't be good. The scale officer shut me down and said, "Son, this mobile home can't be moved again till these winds die down. We do it for your safety, because when they blow like this, we'd have a lot of mobile homes blown over."

I called the home office, and they gave me a terminal agent's number in Cheyenne. They told me to check with him on weather conditions each morning before rolling to make sure it was safe. When I called him, he insisted that I not get a motel, and he proceeded to drive and pick me up. I protested politely when he wanted me to stay with him and his wife, but he wouldn't take "no" for an answer. I ended staying at their home for two days. They treated me like a king and were some of the nicest people you would ever want to meet. After those two days, I was able to head for Utah.

When I got to the Utah scales, they told me that my mobile home tires weren't heavy enough ply tires to cross their state. Down south, we run ten ply tires every day, but here, they required fourteen ply tires. Oh, well, Susan would have to wire more money, or I was stuck again. After about 900 dollars and four hours of running around finding and changing out those tires, I was finally allowed to leave, and I made it to Idaho and delivered. Susan and the broker tried to find me something to pull back home, and I even called the home office. But apparently, in the winter, they don't pull many mobile homes out West. The home office couldn't believe this Arkansas boy had little enough sense to try it in the dead of winter, let alone actually make it.

Coming home on that trip, I almost lost Brownie and my life, too. I came to a mountain pass, and, as I started down the steep grade of that mountain, the road looked clear, but I was so wrong! I had never heard of "black ice," and an empty toter truck unloaded is light on the rear end and near helpless and crippled on "black ice." The farther I went down that mountain, the faster Brownie went. My butt started to draw up, and an eighteen-wheeler behind me hollered out over his CB when he saw me beginning to slide, "Don't hit your brakes, keep gearing down, this is black ice. I drive up here all the time. If you listen and stay cool, we'll get you to the bottom. We don't have much farther till it levels out."

I gripped the wheel; I know I was sweating, but Brownie and I rode it on down. When we got to the bottom, I pulled over and sat there, being thankful for his help. I had been one worried country boy from Arkansas.

The broker kept me pulling all over the United States. In those years, I pulled mobile homes in every state in the United States, except Oregon, Washington, Maine, and Rhode Island. Sometimes, I was gone for eight or nine days at a time. When things are going good, you tend to push bad things to the back side of your brain. Now, either Susan or I had forgotten about owing the IRS those payroll taxes. In fact, we would mail them some money whenever we could. But the interest and penalties on the money we owed them was mounting far faster than we could ever imagine.

One morning, Susan was home raking leaves in our backyard, when a men dressed in a suit and tie pulled into our driveway, got out, and walked up to her while she was raking.

He asked, "Is this where Bobby Henley lives?" She didn't say anything at first, and then he flashed an ID badge and said, "I'm from the IRS. Are you his wife? I need to talk to him about some taxes that are owed."

Now, I guess it just struck Susan the wrong way. She's out there working up a sweat, raking leaves, and this man is interrupting her labors. She looked him in the eye and said, "Bobby isn't here. He has to work for a living, and we're paying you all we can on that tax bill."

That's when the IRS man made his first mistake—he shouldn't have smarted off to Susan. Using an aggressive tone, he said, "Well, you haven't been paying enough to make a dent in what you owe. We might have to 'seize' all your assets."

Boy, was that the wrong thing for him to say to Susan. She threw down that yard rake and said, "Do whatever you will. Seize if you must, this ten-year-old mobile that is financed; my van, which is financed; and Bobby's truck, which is financed. And when you do, be prepared for the U.S. government to feed our seven kids 'cause when you seize everything, we won't be able to make a living and pay you one red cent. Now, get your ass in that car and get off my property, and do it right now."

When she told me what she had done, I came unglued. I knew they wouldn't stop harassing us until they got all their money, and we were doing all we could to pay it back as it was. A week later, a big black man walked into the terminal and asked for Bobby or Susan Henley. Susan invited him into her office, but when he flashed more IRS credentials, she sternly told him to leave. This was her place of business, and she wouldn't discuss personal affairs with him here. He started to argue, but she looked at him and said, "Get out of my workplace right now."

Upon hearing this, I told Susan, "I guess you know you probably pissed them off now. They'll take everything we have, and we'll end up with nothing."

But she looked at me and said, "They don't want a run-down mobile home, a worn-out Chevy van and pickup. Your toter truck is financed, and if they take it, they sure won't get any money, 'cause then you can't work. All those bastards want is money."

That following week, they would begin to get their money, but they would do it their way! The terminal agent called me into the office and presented me a garnishment of wage notice from the IRS. They would now take 75 percent of each of my freight bills turned into the company. By the end of that first week, I realized just how much money they would take from us. I would turn in a freight bill for 400 dollars. The company would first get their 25 percent, any permits for the trip, insurance fees for the trip, and any advance I had drawn. Then the IRS would take 75 percent of that balance. Sometimes, my check for a trip would end up being 21.79 dollars or 13.78 dollars, and even sometimes as little as 1.26 dollars for a smaller trip. At the end of the week, our total checks wouldn't be as much as 200 dollars. That wasn't even enough to buy groceries for our family and pay utilities, and it sure wasn't going to make my 1,300 dollars per month payment on my toter truck. They also sent a tax lien and judgment to the credit bureau. Since I had been sending payments to them from our bank account, they cleaned out every penny from our checking account.

We struggled through for several months like this. I picked up cash labor jobs on the side and managed to make a little extra that the IRS couldn't get their hands on, so we could just survive. It worried me to death, and it was hard to work with this bearing on my mind constantly.

As it got close to Christmas, although Susan never showed how much all this really bothered her, she began to crack. She was crying one night when I came in, and she said to me, "What are we going to do about Christmas for the kids? They will not understand when there are no gifts under the tree. I can take anything but their disappointment. I despise the "Infernal Revenue Service."

I couldn't stand seeing her and my family like this during the holidays. It wasn't the best Christmas we would ever share, but I did manage to make enough that I, she, and our kids enjoyed the holidays. Maybe, I prayed, we could think of a way to pay those taxes, and hopefully next year would be better.

This is another thing that I never fully understood about this whole tax thing—my other partners, who owed their equal portion of these taxes, had different IRS agents assigned to their cases. They plead too much debt and told their agents to come get everything they had, and the IRS never pursued any of the other partners for a portion of the taxes owed. They ended up not paying one dollar toward this debt. I believe that because Susan and I kept sending a little money to them, we became their scapegoat for collecting this money. We were honest and tried to pay a debt we knew was owed by us.

In January, when my truck payment came due, it was evident to me that I didn't have the money to make my payment on my toter truck on time. I had never been late with anyone on anything in my life that I had promised to pay. I called the finance company, and because of my good pay record, they allowed me to make a one time interest payment on my truck. They explained that it was a one-time thing, and I would have to make all future payments in full on time. I was relieved for now and thanked them for their consideration on this matter.

Without a checking account, Susan was running around paying our bills with cash or spending money we didn't have to buy money orders for the ones that had to be mailed. It was driving her and me crazy. A good, young man named Stan, who lived up the street from us, had started driving the truck that Susan had leased to the company when we closed down Homes,

Inc. It hadn't been used much at first because the motor had been bad, and we had to spend money to rebuild it. Since we got it repaired, he had been driving it, and that created a little more income. Stan became a lifesaver with that extra income and one of our dearest friends. He agreed to help us open a checking account under B&S with his name. The money in that account would be ours, but he would sign checks to pay bills and operate in a business manner again. Sometimes, Susan would forget to have Stan sign a check, and she would take a check to buy groceries or pay for our fuel at the fuel stop, or even pay our insurance. She'd just sign Stan's name when that happened and hand them the check. Since everyone knew us so well, they would just smile really big and look at Susan and say, "Thanks so much, Stan. Have a great day!"

It worked okay, but it made Susan and I feel like we didn't really exist anymore. We had lost our identity. We couldn't even sign our own name to a check to pay our bills anymore!

I kept working as hard as I could. I was gone for days at a time on those long trips. When we were pulling and selling all those repos several years ago, Susan and I had managed to setup about fifteen repos on lots in our subdivision as rental units. We had several of them paid for now, and so far, the IRS had not found out about them. Susan was determined to get us out from under this debt anyway she could. What she did, unbeknown to me, was when a renter would move out of one of our rentals—which was paid for—she would advertise it for sale for cash and sell it. She would buy a cashier's check, and send the money to the IRS.

While I came home one night really late and totally exhausted, she told me, "Honey, I sold a bunch of our rental units while you were gone on this trip. I've been doing this for a while. Today, I sent the IRS a cashier's check for the balance we owed them—10,000 dollars. I don't know how long it will take for them to release the garnishment with the company, but it's paid in full."

A huge weight had been lifted from me, and a feeling of relief passed over me. In two years, Susan and I had ended paying the "United States Infernal Revenue Service" over 93,000 dollars in taxes, penalties, and interest. Maybe you think I misspelled the work "Internal," but to Susan and me they were the "Infernal" Revenue Service.

Chapter Six
Politics—Changing the Law

While anxiously waiting for the release of my garnishment, Susan's driver and Stan, moved a mobile home from Alexander, Arkansas to Springfield, Missouri for a couple. They headed up Highway 65 in Arkansas, which, at that time, was a crooked and narrow two-lane highway. Because of the road conditions, all mobile home transporters in Arkansas hated that road and tried to avoid going that way at all costs. But going to Springfield from where we started was our closest and best route to travel. Stan was an excellent escort and would wave that red stick flag in the face of oncoming drivers when needed to make them pull over. But today would put his escort ability to the ultimate test.

As the mobile home driver rounded a curve, he saw Stan waving that red stick flag and flashing his lights. As our driver approached the center of a narrow bridge, Stan started yelling over the CB, "There's an old couple in a big motor home pulling a little car, and they aren't slowing down. They were coming around the curve and down the hill so fast that I couldn't get them to stop. They're going to meet you before you get off that bridge."

Stan was right, because just as our driver exited the bridge with only our truck, the couple in that motor home hit the front corner of the mobile home, taking with them metal siding and wall studs, and scattering our customer's clothing from the front bedroom closet all over the road and down into the water of the creek bed below the bridge.

Stan called to let me know what just had happened, and Susan and I took off to the accident site as soon as we could. We were assured by Stan that no one was injured badly, but the mobile home we were pulling, and the couple's motor home had extensive damage. The highway police investigated, and I learned something new from this experience. All wide loads are considered totally at fault even with flashing lights, wide load signs, and red flags waving if over a center line of a highway. Even if the escort and the driver warned the oncoming traveler to slow down or pull over for them, this would be an insurance claim against Susan's driver's driving record. The company would be liable for all damages. The company would have to pay for the mobile home and the motor home to settle this insurance claim.

To make matters worse, the media somehow got involved in this accident. Two days later, as Brownie and I pulled into the terminal, the Channel 7 television station news crew stood taking pictures of *my* truck and I as we rolled in. I tried to explain that I was not in any way involved in this accident with my truck, but they refused to listen. That night, the television station aired the report of an accident between a mobile home and a motor home, which included a picture of Brownie and I in the background. I guess I should have pursued this more and made them rescind or revise their story, but I didn't. For weeks after that, everywhere I went, I was asked if I was that driver who wrecked that mobile home up Highway 65 near Marshall, Arkansas. I ended up explaining that I wasn't involved to a lot of people whom I did business with for quite a while after that.

On a happier note, the release arrived at the terminal, stating that my taxes had been paid in full and no more garnishments could be withheld from my checks. I don't think there has been anything in this business that had worried me more. My hands had been tied for a long time and I sure wouldn't want the U.S. government to miss any money they could collect from the little guy. I knew I owed them, and I paid them every penny.

The broker from Texas called and had a double-wide building for a church going from Houston, Texas to Long Island, New York. Of course, I wanted this trip because it paid over 20,000 dollars. I called my brother, and he agreed to go with me and pulled half of the mobile home. Our escorts on this trip were Joker and Mule. We made good time, and in a couple of days, arrived on Saturday near Pittsburg, Pennsylvania just before dark at a truck stop. After backing our mobile home into a safe spot on the parking lot, we jumped into the two escort trucks and reserved motel rooms. We then headed for the truck stop restaurant to get a good hot meal, but on the way in, Mule bumped into a big, burly truck driver. He tried to start an argument with Mule, but Mule told him, "Man, I'm really sorry. I didn't mean to bump into you."

The truck driver finally walked away, cussing and grumbling under his breath. I told Mule to ignore him and sit on down and order his food. While we waited for our food to come, Mule said, "I've got to go to the restroom. I'll be right back."

Well, Joker couldn't resist this opportunity and said, "Come on, let's get Mule. Follow me."

I followed Joker into the restroom, and Mule was in a stall with his pants down around his ankles, sitting on the "throne."

Joker started kicking and pounding on the stall door, hollering, "I think I'll just kick your ass right now for bumping into me!"

That's when the commotion started. Joker hid behind another stall door. Mule ran out of his stall, jerking his pants up as he went, and almost knocked me down as he headed out that bathroom door. I heard him say while running and looking back toward me, "That guy is going to kick my ass. He's starting crap with me in the damn restroom."

Needless to say, it took Joker and me several minutes to compose ourselves from our laughter before we could return to our table.

Since we can't pull mobile homes on Sunday, we had to stay all day and the next night at that motel and truck stop. Now, this was a huge truck stop, and unfortunately, it was frequented by a lot of prostitutes, trying to take money from the truck drivers.

One of the prostitutes' CB handle was "Sugar Britches," and every time we leave our room to go and eat, we would hear Sugar Britches on the CB radio, asking, "Is there any man out there looking for a good time?"

Well, Mule listened to this all day, and when we left the restaurant that night, as we headed back to our room, he just couldn't resist asking any longer, "Hey, Sugar Britches, this is the Mule, how much do you charge?"

My brother and Mule were in one truck, and Joker and I in another. When she didn't answer back for Mule, I couldn't help but respond. I got on my CB and answered back to Mule for her, "Hey, Mule, it's Sugar Britches. Where are you, baby?"

Mule hurried and replied, "I'm heading over to room 104, baby. Where are you?"

I answered him back, trying to sound like a woman without laughing. "Mule, stand outside your room. I'll drive over and get a good look at you, baby."

As luck would have it, there happened to be several cars and trucks pulling in and out of the motel lot at this time. When Joker and I drove past Mule's room, there he stood outside, smoking a cigarette, looking all around, while trying to look cool at the same time. I waited a few minutes and got back on my CB to say, "Oh, my gosh, Mule. You're way too ugly for me!"

Joker and I were laughing so hard. I don't know how I even managed to say that without giving us away. But, then, we heard Mule shout, "Screw you, Sugar Britches."

We never told Mule it was Joker and I playing a joke on him until we headed back home several days later.

On Monday, we pulled out, headed for Long Island, and stopped to eat lunch on the New Jersey state line at a truck stop called Mini Skirt Junction. All the waitresses wore short black miniskirts. We never got to eat our lunch because Joker harassed the waitresses. He pinched one on the rear and got us thrown out of the place. They just didn't appreciate the Joker's good ole boy pranks.

When we crossed over into New York near the city, we learned that no wide loads were allowed through the toll booths into the city without an appointment. Also, we would need to call for police escorts to cross the city to Long Island. And by the way, we couldn't cross until night because of traffic. At our scheduled appointment time, our police escorts arrived and led us through the toll booth. The route would take us down through the Bronx. The police told us to follow them and don't make any stops for lights or stop signs; just keep close to them. This old country boy would never have imagined the reality of the Bronx if I hadn't experienced it firsthand. This was during the garbage strike in New York, and the sanitation workers hadn't picked up any trash for nearly a week at this time.

As we moved along behind the police cars down those streets, city trash had been piled up against the tenement buildings on the sidewalks and spilling out into the streets in some place over a full story tall. Battered and stripped cars sat abandoned on the curbs against this rotting mess. At one corner, off in the shadows, I witnessed a man with a gun pointed at another man. A young boy jumped up on the hood of Mule's escort truck, and he insisted to wash our windshield for five dollars. All the while, Mule and I were rolling as fast as we can without running over our police escort. We were never so glad to exit the Bronx and see Long Island.

I keep telling Susan, even today, that I would like to take her to New York City, and each time, she politely replies, after our stories of this trip, "Thanks, but no thanks! I have no desire to go there."

During this summer my son, Chris, and Susan's son, Bud, wanted to help me so they could make some spending money. One hot morning, I had a mobile home to move close to our house and decided to take both boys with me. Grass and weeds had grown up near knee-deep around this mobile home. It took us a while to weed eat up close to the mobile home before we could actually begin working. Now, every time I looked up from working and getting this mobile home ready, those two boys would be constantly picking and playing, instead of trying to help in the work. I scolded them and told them to get to work. I crawled up under the mobile home to secure a bad area in the floor, where the water heater had leaked and rotted the floor out and left a hole. I knew that if it wasn't secured when I pulled down the road, the water heater could fall out. I was laying flat of my back, looking up, working on this when those two boys played another prank. They thought of how funny it would be like to drop a little dead snake they found down that hole, on top of my face and head. Now, I'm not afraid of many things, but I would rather have the devil after me than a *snake!*

When that snake fell on my face, I struggled to get away, bumped my bald head on the iron frame of that mobile home, and came out swiftly, with my hammer in hand. By then, both of those boys were laughing hysterically. But it wasn't a damn bit funny to me, because, dead or alive, *I hate a snake.* Hammer in hand and madder than hell, I chased those two boys almost a block down that street, threatening their lives before I calmed down. They are both lucky I didn't catch up on them sooner than I did, because I might have hurt them badly.

On another trip in late summer, Bud went with me to South Padre Island, Texas. He had never been to the ocean, and to him it would be like a small vacation. It was a hot, sultry day when we arrived close to the beach. I had already realized I wouldn't get any work done until I drove him over to that beach and let him see the ocean. Being a hot-blooded young man of seventeen, I soon realized that the ocean wasn't what he was looking at. His eyes were traveling from one scanty bikini clad young girl to another. I didn't blame him for gazing. I wasn't seventeen anymore, but I surely liked the scenery on that beach, too.

Back to work, we had a job to get done! It was 117 degrees that day, and our customer was very cordial, trying to keep us from getting too hot. She asked what we liked to drink and Bud told her that he loved Dr. Pepper. She returned in short order with a huge ice chest with drinks. Bud wasn't at all used to these humid, hot temperatures, especially working out in them. Every few minutes, I would see him pausing from his work, opening that lid on her ice chest, and gulping down a cold Dr. Pepper. I was conditioned to work in the heat, and I knew you don't keep on drinking ice cold drinks like that. That boy drank seventeen Dr. Peppers one right after another before I knew it. His head was soon dizzy, and he told me he didn't feel very well. Imagine that!

I had to finish the mobile home by myself while he sat with his head hung down, not looking very well at all. On the trip home, he told me, "I don't believe I want to become a mobile home mover. When I finish high school, if it won't make you mad, I think I will go to college and do something else with my life."

I tried not to grin at him when I said, "No, son, it won't make me mad. This business is hard work, sometimes under unbearable conditions. Not everyone is cut out for it. I think you might want to get your education."

And with that advice, he lay his head over on the door and slept his sugary sickness off as we headed toward home.

Now, on all these long trips, even with all the fun we had, I kept in my mind how much money I was making Transit Homes of America, Inc. Over the past three years, I had worked my tail off and given a big part of my earnings back to the company. I never did understand about that 1950 law in Arkansas. It just wasn't right that I couldn't have my own company and work in my own state. On that long drive back from New York, I had told my brother, "Somehow, I'm going to get that law changed."

He just had laughed and said, "Sure you are," and forgot about it.

But I had made up my mind. It was time to get rid of this nearly fifty-year-old law. I was going to work on getting it changed one way or the other!

One morning, I got up and told Susan, "I'm going to the state capital and talk to my state senators and representatives about that crazy law. I don't know where to begin, but I have to try." Each morning, I arrived at the state capital for over a week. I went to as many offices of senators and representatives as I could, but I was getting nowhere fast. I could talk to secretaries and assistants, but I have to have an appointment to see a senator or representative. I walked up and down those marble steps until my cowboy boots put blisters on my every toe. At recess, between sessions of the state congress, I stopped senators and tried to tell them my story about this law. When I insisted it was time to get it changed, most of them were polite enough to listen. But I could tell, when they shook my hand and walked away, that I had not gotten their attention on how unfair this old law was.

One morning, during a recess, I was fortunate enough to see the senator from my old district, who I knew, talking to several other senators in the hallway. They were laughing and having a good time. I decided to boldly walk up and speak to him. He greeted me and shook hand and asked, "Hello, Bobby! What are you doing at the state capital?"

I briefly explained my quest to him, and he said, "We're all about to go to the buffet luncheon. Come and join us, and we'll have time to talk about it with several of my constituents."

While I ate lunch beside him, he introduced me to everyone in the room, and they actually began listening to my story. Most of them didn't even know this old law existed. My senator told them it sounded very unconstitutional that a young, hard working man, like myself, was being deprived the right to work in his own state. Some wondered why I would even attempt to challenge the change of such a law. I never imagined that anything would be done, but at least I had been heard that day. Before that lunch was over, several senators shook my hand, all the time agreeing they would check into this law. I had no idea how much support or opposition they would get on the idea of changing it, but I had a little hope now.

After several weeks, a bill was presented to remove this law from the state of Arkansas. It was in essence a bill to deregulate intrastate authority for mobile homes in Arkansas. Its passage would give anyone the right to apply and be granted the right for intrastate authority to move mobile homes. The opposition protested this bill fiercely, just as I knew they would, and fought hard against it being passed. They knew that if this bill passed, I would only be one of many mobile homes transporters to file for their own authority and work for themselves. There were a lot more mobile home drivers out there who despised this denial of their right to work for themselves in our state.

But in the end, enough votes were in favor to change this law. I had started this journey, and I had won! Intrastate authority to move mobile homes in Arkansas would now be granted to anyone able to meet the guidelines and criteria as outlined in the new bill. I intended to be and was the first one to file and be granted this authority upon this bill's passage. Others would soon follow behind me. Very few mobile home transporters ever knew until now that I, Bobby Henley, was in fact an important key that got this law changed in our great state. *You* can change the course of politics and have a voice if only you are brave enough to *speak out*!

Chapter Seven
All on My Own "Finally" Again

Finally, everything I do in the mobile home business will be all mine. I don't have any partners to answer to or any nationwide corporation taking a part of my money. The IRS will never be able to seize anything I have if it's the last thing I do. It was like a huge burden had been lifted off my shoulders. Sadly enough, though, I would miss my relationship with Transit Homes of America, Inc. Even with the slow start I had with the company, I had emerged as one of their most trusted and income producing drivers every year. I became friends with the owner and his wife, but shortly after I terminated my lease, they sold the company for several million dollars. Who knows what changes I might have been enduring with new corporate owners?

Now, Susan and I could concentrate on us by accomplishing what she and I really wanted from this life, with our business providing the means. Even with all our hardship and struggles, we had managed to buy a little farm from an older couple, who took a chance and owner-financed it for us. We managed to assume a loan on a house next to it with more acreage. The house was not finished inside, and for our large family, we would need to add another bedroom. But for now, maybe we could make enough money to afford sheetrock, plumbing, paint, carpet, and appliances, so we could actually move in.

The mobile home dealer in Missouri was the first one to give us a new beginning. He wanted us to go and get a double-wide repo from a dealer lot in Montpelier, Vermont. I called my brother, and we decided not to leave until after New Year's Day. My brother and I shared whatever work he or I had with each other for many years. After all, he's the one who got me started in the business.

Sadly, Miss Butterscotch had become ill and passed away during the Christmas holiday. My brother called Joker to escort him. Susan had never been to the northeast before and begged to go with me. We left on January 2 and headed for Vermont. Just north of Nashville, Tennessee, it started sleeting and snowing. At first, for several hundred miles, it was barely spitting frozen stuff off and on. But soon, it became apparent that it was wintertime in the northeast. In order to save fuel, we had tow bars on the front of the escorts and towed them behind the toter trucks. We drove through some heavy snow all day, and, late that afternoon, were exhausted from fighting the road conditions. We were somewhere in New York State and found a small motel to get a room. The room wasn't much, but we knew we were too tired to go any farther. By now, the temperature outside was fourteen degrees and the snow and winds were howling. All our diesel trucks had a plug-in on the motors to keep the engines from freezing, so we ran our extension cord to an outlet in our motel room for the night. We also poured an additive in the fuel to help prevent it from freezing. We tried to get some sleep, but the radiator heaters in our room barely warmed the room to forty degrees all night long. It was an unbearable sleeping condition. I think we were all relieved when morning finally arrived, so we could crank up the heaters on our trucks and try to get warm. But the temperature outside overnight had dropped below zero degrees, and my brother's truck would not start. Brownie and my escort truck grunted at first, but kicked off and started. We worked for four hours using every means we could think of on my brother's toter, until we finally resorted to running the hair dryer on the fuel lines. Finally, after a few minutes of up close heat, it got started. What a mess, now we would have a late night getting to Vermont!

Upon arriving in Vermont and finding a room with heat, we got a restful night's sleep. We found the dealer lot with our double-wide early the next morning, but the winter storm had preceded us there. There was over two feet of ice and snow piled on its roof. Now, we would have to buy shovels and remove the ice and snow before we could even separate the two halves and get it ready to pull. Usually, Susan would jump in and help get a mobile home ready, but in ten-degree weather with snow and ice, all I could get her to do was look out the window of the dealer's heated office with compassion as we worked. Joker wasn't much help in these conditions either. He preferred staying in there with Susan. Finally, late that afternoon, chilled to the bone and skin nearly frost-bitten, we were ready to roll and could head home the next morning.

In Albany, New York, Susan was escorting me and read our permit route wrong. Before having time to realize it, she was escorting Brownie and me, with the others following suit, through downtown Albany with cars parked on both sides of those narrow city streets, pedestrians pointing and staring in awe, and traffic lights at every corner hanging too low. It was a really slow go not to bump a parked car or rub the shingles on that roof at each intersection on those traffic lights. Just as we made a turn and think we're in the clear, we turned to exit downtown Albany. And there was a barricade over an open manhole with a city worker sticking out of it. Luckily, before the city police were called, he moved the barricade. We straddled the manhole and managed to leave this quaint town.

We only traveled another thirty-nine miles before dark caught us. We found a truck stop to park and a motel room for the night. At breakfast the next morning, it started to snow again a little. We hurriedly left with our mobile home and got on the road again. The farther we went, the bigger the snowflakes were. At one point, they looked as big as saucers, and when they would hit the windshield, they would splatter like eggs in a hot skillet. The snow was a mixture of heavy snowflakes, ash, salt, and sand spread on the road by the highway department to try and keep the roads from closing down. My next hour was spent hollering at Susan on the CB radio to "Go on," and her hollering back at me, "I'm going as fast as I intend on going. I've used up all my windshield wiper fluid. My windshield is a big blurry mess. I can't see the road."

By now, the snow on the roads was deep, and they were treacherous. I was starting to get worried about the conditions myself. I knew that if Susan got scared in front of me because she couldn't see the road and slowed down or stopped, Brownie and I would run over the top of her. Enough was enough of this. When a truck driver told us on his CB that they were shutting down the road ahead of us going east, I told Susan, "We are almost to Rocky Top, Pennsylvania. Watch for an exit ramp. We're getting off this mess before one of us gets hurt!"

Within a very few minutes, I saw Susan go right off the exit ramp. It's a good thing because they closed the roads just a few minutes after our exit.

On top of Rocky Top, there was a truck stop, a small motel, a grocery store, and a laundry mat. Now, we had planned on delivering in Missouri today and headed toward home, with it being Friday. All our clothes were dirty; we were tired of the snow; our money was running low; the motel room with two beds was tiny, and we were irritable; and we're stuck in Rocky Top, on this snow-covered mountain at least for the whole weekend, with too much togetherness! It was snowing each morning when we would wake up and get ready for breakfast. By Saturday noon, Joker and my brother were all sulky and refused to go eat with Susan and me at the truck stop restaurant. They were whining about sitting there stranded, losing more and more money on this trip.

When we finished eating our lunch, Susan walked over to the grocery store and brought back Vienna sausages, crackers, cheese, and apples. It only stirred them up more when she emptied the sack of groceries on their bed and said, "I don't want you big babies to starve while we are here."

They really protested when she next informed them to give her all their quarters and their dirty underwear and clothes. She said she was going to the laundry mat, so they wouldn't stink. She had them so steamed up by now that neither of them ate at the restaurant with us the rest of the weekend or breakfast that

Monday morning when we got the "all roads are clear" message from truck drivers.

When we rolled into Benton, Missouri on Monday afternoon, Joker and my brother, still sulking, unhooked their mobile home at the dealer's lot and started to drive away. I hollered at them to wait, so we could stop at the throw rolls restaurant and eat some of those good hot rolls. I told them to give me a few minutes to collect our money from the dealer. They never slowed down, stopped, waited, or answered me. I told Susan, "I guess they're too tight to stop and eat a good meal. Forget them, we're stopping to eat."

I guess I thought I should make up for them not stopping. I enjoyed five of those big, heavy, buttered yeast rolls with my meal before Susan and I headed home.

My dad, Slowpoke, had been escorting my brother and me for about two years. He was dependable even though he couldn't work fast anymore. I knew that his hearing wasn't really good anymore, and his sight was starting to fail him, too. But he loved to go with his sons on these long trips. I knew what was about to happen, but I didn't know it would be like this.

Our next trip for the dealer in Missouri was a mobile home from Kenosha, Wisconsin. I called Slowpoke, and he said, "Stop by and I'll have my pickup fueled and ready to go with you."

Our route south, down I-94 into Chicago, took us by O'Hare International Airport. My dad and I had never seen anything like O'Hare before. We pulled over in a safe spot for several minutes, watching in amazement at what seemed like a thousand planes of all sizes and descriptions taking off and landing. They were everywhere in the skies above us. After we pulled out and started rolling again, Slowpoke talked for miles about O'Hare. As we traveled out of Chicago, there were a lot of road construction up ahead, and orange barrels were lining the roadway. I hollered at Slowpoke, "I'll have to go slow through here. I don't want to bump this mobile home on one of those barrels."

A couple of cars and eighteen-wheelers had gotten between Slowpoke and I, and I couldn't see his taillights anymore on the escort. He wasn't answering me, and I knew he had gotten too far in front of me to hear me on the CB radio. I thought, *Oh, well, I'll just ease along and catch up to him.* I kept trying to get him to answer as I went. One truck driver even told me that he saw him not far up ahead. I still had no reason to worry.

As the construction area ended, I pulled off shortly after that in a truck stop. I was thinking he would be sitting there in the parking lot, watching, and waiting for me...but he was not there and still would not answer me on the radio. It was getting dark, and I was starting to worry about him. I called Susan and asked, "Has Daddy called you? We got separated in a construction zone, and he won't answer me on the radio. I hope he doesn't have truck troubles."

Susan had not heard from him. I told her I would unhook my toter from the mobile home and drive back north. If he had broken down, I would find him. I drove all the way back to where the construction had started, constantly looking for a sign of him. When I called Susan back and she had not heard from him, I knew I should call Mama.

When I called her, she said, "No, I haven't talked to him. What do you mean you can't find him? How could he get lost with you following him?"

Now, Mama would be upset and worried until I found Daddy. For the next six to eight hours, I drove and looked for him. I called Susan. I called Mama. I stopped at truck stops and gas stations, and I talked on my CB radio constantly. No one had seen Daddy!

Finally, one truck driver hollered on his CB radio, "Hey, hand, I think I saw your escort truck about forty-three miles south at a truck stop. It sure sounds like the pickup you are describing."

I had no other choice but to head south. I pulled into the parking lot, and in front of the truck stop restaurant sat my escort vehicle. I went inside and looked about until I spotted Slowpoke at a table. I tried not to be disrespectful. When I asked him, "What are you doing? I've been looking for you for nearly eight hours."

He pushed his glasses down on his nose as he looked over them and said, "Ah, son, I knew you'd come find me eventually. I just ordered some breakfast and coffee. I got hungry."

Susan and Mama had been up all night talking to me, wondering and waiting for news about Daddy. I called them and assured them that the old fart was okay.

When we got home from that trip, I told Susan that what I had to do was going to be hard. This trip just iced the cake. It was time to retire Slowpoke from driving. I knew it would break his heart, and I truly hated to tell him, but he could not go with us anymore. He couldn't hear, he couldn't see, and he was going to get one of us or himself hurt. He didn't take the news very well, but I knew it was the right thing to do.

After that trip to Vermont, my brother refused to go on any more of those long trips. He told me that the expense was too great, and too many unforeseen things could happen, decreasing the profits. The dealer in Jacksonville who gave me a chance with Transit Homes of America, Inc. had opened up four sales lots. The new mobile home sales were increasing, and we both decided to stay at home and work in Arkansas. My brother lived closer to the two lots in Jacksonville and Searcy, and we decided he would move their homes. I would move homes for the Pine Bluff and Hot Springs sales lots.

Susan and I loved the huge money those long trips generated. But every time I would get ready to leave (especially with her knowing I would be gone several days), I would have to drive off leaving her crying. She hated me being gone on those trips, and I didn't want to leave her that way. Work was good near home again, so I could stay closer to home and cuddle up to my wife each night, which made both of us happier.

The sales lot in Pine Bluff had very ambitious sales people working there, and they were selling homes faster than I could deliver them. Brownie and I still hold what I think is a mobile home delivery record. In one day, we delivered six mobile homes to customer locations, and my crews got all of them but one setup. We were making more money at home than I could have ever imagined. The dealer suggested making even more money for both of us. I should buy another toter truck. My brother could seldom help me now. He had his hands full with the other two sales lots.

I inquired with a company about another truck in Kansas City, Missouri. They specialized in eighteen-wheeler trucks that were reconditioned, had low miles, and had been converted into mobile home toter trucks. They faxed pictures of one of the trucks they had just reconditioned and sent a price on it. My middle son, John, had started helping me, and I knew he was ready to drive and start pulling mobile homes.

Susan and I loaded into one of our pickups on Friday and headed for Missouri. The truck was super sharp, had low miles, and, unlike Brownie, had a new six-way hitch and hydraulic mirrors. You could operate the hitch and mirrors to any position with a push of a button from inside the cab of the truck. The salesman got financing approved while we waited, and I drove our new purchase home with Susan close behind in the pickup. I was like a kid with a new toy at Christmas!

I drove the new truck for a few weeks, loving all the new modern gadgets it had to help make moving a mobile home a lot easier. But this truck was a lot heavier on the front end than Brownie, and I found myself getting stuck a lot more than I was accustomed to. My son, John, wasn't getting along very well driving Brownie. He was jealous of me driving that new truck and found some reason every day to complain about Brownie. I finally got tired of hearing him moan and groan. I relinquished that new truck to him to drive, and I got my butt back in Brownie. Brownie was starting to have a few minor problems, but I knew just how to handle that old truck. I knew that if John kept on driving it, he wouldn't keep him running enough to work.

Brownie and I went one day for this dealer to get a double-wide repo. When I got there and approached the mobile home, I knew this one would be a real challenge. For two years, the customer had lived in this home with no sewer line connected. Open sewage had been allowed to run out on the ground under the mobile home and was piled up nearly two feet deep.

At first, the ground looked like it was dry and hard, but everywhere you stepped, your feet would break through that top, dry shallow crust of sewage. And it would break through to the worst stinking, nasty mess you can imagine. We would have to lay in that mess to hang axles and wheels on the mobile home and jack it up to unblock it. Now, my crew was loyal and faithful on most of my jobs, but they balked about lying in human crap. I agreed with them, but I knew we had to get this home. We bought sheets of plywood and plastic sheeting to lie on the ground, so we could get under there and work. As we would lay down on our makeshift platforms, human sewage would ooze out around us and start to run onto the plastic and plywood where we lay working. I wanted to drive off and refuse this job several times, but *need to work*, kept me there. The stench was terrible, and I'm lying there in this mess, wondering how can any human live in these unsanitary conditions.

The next day, we went back for more torture to try and get this repo. We took a bulldozer, more sheets of plywood, railroad ties, and iron mats to try and keep the mobile home from breaking through the crust as we buried up to our knees in this crap for hours to get it to the street. When it was finally on the street, if you can imagine the stench of ourselves with this stinking mess combined with sweat from our labors, we stripped off our clothes and changed right there in the street. If you think I cared who saw me standing there near naked changing into cleaner clothes, you would be wrong! There was no way I would ride in Brownie, even with the windows down, smelling like I did. That night at home, I didn't even think one shower would be enough to get me clean again. I guess this might be one of the worst repos I have ever done.

About two months after I bought the new truck, the dealer called me into his office one morning to have a talk. Since the mobile home business was booming now, it seemed everyone had bought a toter truck and was out to get a piece of this action. They had been paying an average of 25,000 dollars per week for deliveries, and I remember one week when Susan collected over 42,000 dollars from them. We had paid off the farm in full, and finished our house and moved in. But on this morning, the dealer shattered our dreams. He said, "I know you have done a lot of homes for us, but the owners have decided to try and cut down their setup and delivery expense. Another transporter has agreed to deliver our homes for a lot less money than you charge. You're going to have to cut your prices, or I'll be forced to use someone who charges us less."

I couldn't believe what he was telling me. I just went into debt for 36,000 dollars for another truck to cover their jobs. Was this really happening? I knew I was already charging them a very fair price for all of the work they gave us. I looked at him and said, "Man, I just bought that new truck because of you and your work. I'll have to give this some thought overnight and get back to you."

I had busted a gut giving service above and beyond to these people. Add up the money! If they were paying me those huge checks each week, how much money had I helped them make? As I drove home, I thought, *Is there no loyalty in this business?* Apparently, there is not, when it comes to the dollar!

The next morning, I gave the dealer my answer. I graciously told him, "I've really enjoyed working for you folks. I've went above and beyond to be honest and faithful to you, but I can't and won't lower my prices to meet the other transporter's prices. Good luck. And if things don't work out, call me." I collected my check for that week, and quietly but respectfully hurt at the outcome, I walked out.

About a week later, the manager for all the sales lots called me to drive to Hot Springs. He said, "I know you've been shafted, and I'm sorry about everything, but the owners are money hungry. But, please, listen and consider what I'm about to tell you. It seems that the other transporter they hired at Pine Bluff doesn't want to drive over here to work. He says it's too far for him. Now, we need someone to deliver our homes over here."

I just looked over the desk at him and didn't say anything for a few minutes. Silently, I was telling myself, *Don't lose your cool, you do need this work.*

Finally, when I decided to answer him, I said, "I will do your work, but I won't lower my prices to do it. I will charge the same thing I always have. If you want that, then we have a deal. But if not, I understand your position." He gave me the long speech about how I had been wronged, and he understood how faithful and loyal I had been at Pine Bluff. I hope I made the right decision as we shook hands and I left.

During this time, another Christmas holiday season came. On Christmas Eve, early in the afternoon, I got a frantic call from my youngest brother. Something bad had happened to my other brother. He was sitting in his den, relaxing after a long day of last minute Christmas shopping, drinking a cup of coffee, and just stopped breathing. He was en route to a hospital in an ambulance. I couldn't believe what I was hearing. I looked at Susan, and she knew something terrible had just happened. I said, "They just took my brother by ambulance to the hospital. We've got to go now, it sounds bad."

When we arrived, it was too late to say good-bye to my brother and best friend in the whole world. They had not been able to save his life. This holiday season was nothing but a dark, sad blur. We got through it as best we could for all the younger children in our family, but it was so difficult. My brother had gotten me in this business, and we had worked together in it for twenty years. I talked to him every day, and he was the last phone call I got, for at least an hour, each night. For months at night, every time my phone would ring, I would reach for it, thinking it was him calling. I had already lost Mama, but I still miss my brother to this day. At his funeral, so many mobile home people filled the chapel to pay their last respects. It was standing room only both inside and out. He was well respected by all in this business!

Two years and about one hundred fifty homes later, the lot at Hot Springs changed managers. The new manager was not as easy to get along with and began conveniently disappearing when it came time to collect our money. I decided it was time to ease slowly out of this business relationship before Susan and I get burned again.

These four lots had been very good to me. For nearly five years, they had paid me an average of 500,000 dollars per year. I hated to see this account go, but in my mind, I knew it was time. I had managed to start moving a lot of individual's homes and was now working with a national leasing company in moving their office buildings. Sometimes being all on your own again is tough!

Chapter Eight
Katrina! and Office Buildings

I guess I forgot to tell something in the last chapter. Brownie had been a dependable and faithful partner for me now for over twenty years. He was requiring quarts of oil every day, puffed white smoke every time I started him, and I had suffered through most of winter with no heat in his cab. But I couldn't bear the thought of driving him down the road with no air conditioning when it got hot weather. It was time to retire my most loyal business partner, whose odometer had stopped working over four years back, with mileage registered on the dashboard at over 800,000. I parked Brownie in the work yard without any thought that I would ever drive him again. I bought another more modern truck with the same commodities and gadgets as the one my son was driving.

    My son had long about now decided that I wasn't paying him enough money for his labors. In the last year he worked for me, I only paid him 72,000 dollars, which I thought was good wages, since I furnished all the fuel, permits, insurance, and paid for all truck repairs. That was his take home pay after all expenses! But I told Susan, "I won't argue with my kids about money. Give me the title to the truck he drives." We signed the title over to him and told him he was now officially on his own in the mobile home business.

My youngest son, Dennis, at about this same time, had decided that high school was not his cup of tea. I would send him to school and barely before the morning bell would ring, the principal's office would call and tell Susan that he wasn't in class *again*. She would call me, and I would tell her to go find him and take him back to school. He wasn't ever hard to find. He always ended up at the same friend's house. That boy should have also been in school. After doing this several times, Susan told me, "We're fighting a losing battle. He is not going to go to school. I'm tired of hauling him back there."

I tried to reason with him when I got home, but he was adamant about not going to school. I still feel like I am partly at fault for him not finishing school, because I let him work that summer, and he had gotten a good taste of how well this business paid. I finally relented and told him that if he would get a GED diploma, I would let him quit school and he could work for me. He did get his diploma and later went into business on his own with my blessings.

I concentrated for several months on acquiring a huge account to move office buildings for two major leasing companies. I believe that most of you have seen those small metal job trailers on new construction sites in your area.

Contractors lease them for a period of time for an office on the job site while building permanent structures. When their structure is built and their lease is finished, I also get to go and return them to the leasing company.

Soon, the leasing company (based in Tulsa, Oklahoma) asked us to deliver and setup double-wide classrooms, while schools were remodeled or expanding their campus. As Indian casinos started up all over Oklahoma, we took double-wide, triple-wide, and as big as ten-section office buildings for them until permanent casino buildings could be built. At first, my son, Dennis, went with me on these setups and worked as hard as I did to please these leasing companies. He was still young and had a lot more to learn, but all in all, he handled the work professionally. Before long, both I and the leasing companies were confident enough to put him in charge of our office building setup crew. He could manage the total setup without me supervising him.

Work was plentiful and construction was booming. Our mobile home office building account was huge. I and my son-in-law, who had started driving another truck, couldn't keep up with all the work. As you can tell by now, this mobile home business is either feast or famine in times of a slow or growing economy. Sue's oldest daughter was dating a young man who was a good driver, and he came to me needing a job. I wasn't about to give up my truck for someone else to drive, but I did the only thing that I could come up with at the time. Brownie was still sitting out there in the work yard, resting in peace, where I had parked him several years ago. Occasionally, I would turn the key and his motor would grunt a little, but then start and sputter a few minutes before I turned the key off. How could I even dare to think about what I was about to do? It was a crazy idea, but I'd done things a lot crazier than what I decided to do.

I called my sister-in-law and asked her to sell me my brother's toter truck. He had just installed a rebuilt motor in it before he unexpectedly passed away. His son had tried to pull mobile homes with it a little, but wasn't mature enough to handle the pressure of this business. I knew that the motor would work in Brownie. We made a deal on the truck, and, within a week, that motor was sitting, ready to go back to work under Brownie's hood. With my daughter's boyfriend behind the wheel, Brownie was "on the road again." Little did I, my crews, or Brownie know what was about to come!

For days, the weather forecasters had been talking about a hurricane out in the Gulf. At first, we paid little attention. After all, it was hurricane season. Every year, several storms managed to grow into hurricanes, and sometimes damage was done somewhere along one of the U.S. coastlines. But soon, everyone everywhere was paying attention to this storm they had named Katrina. The night before she was due to hit landfall, weather forecasters were stressing the magnitude of this storm and predicting it to be a Category 5, the very worst hurricane possible, when it hit. It looked like it would hit somewhere around New Orleans, but when it did, none of us could imagine the horrible, devastation that would be left behind. For several days, then several weeks, every channel on every TV was filled with horrifying, unrealistic pictures. All of you remember what they looked like. Our whole nation was in total disbelief at what our southern coastline was enduring!

One week after this disaster, my phones were ringing off the wall. My office leasing companies were calling me asking, "How many trucks do you have? When can you get here? How many setup crews can you get together?" The fax machine was filled with urgent requests to get mobile office buildings from Tulsa, Oklahoma City, St. Louis, Dallas, Memphis, and Kansas City. They had to get these buildings to the coast as soon as possible, and, of course, we were ready to help.

The number one priority was to get seven double-wides to Gulfport for NOAA right on the ocean front. This was easier said than done. Roadways were still blocked with trees or portions of them totally gone. Homes, huge boats, steel beams, cars, and some things so large and twisted—we didn't recognize what they had been before—seemed to block our path in every direction. The pictures on TV had not prepared us in any way for what we really saw in our journey to get to the coast. For two weeks, we weaved our way through all manner of debris; roadblocks by the national guards; stations with no electricity to allow us to get more fuel in our trucks; no running water to use the restroom; and no motel rooms or restaurants to stop and eat a meal into on these trips within 250 miles from Gulfport. Gulfport was unrecognizable to me anymore, and most of it didn't exist now.

Once we delivered these double-wides, I wondered where my setup crew would sleep, and how they would eat when they got there to work. I called Susan and told her, "Find us a good used travel trailer to bring down here and a generator for power. Our boys can't stay down here for three or four weeks and work. There is nothing here; it's all gone or ruined."

That was easier said than done, though. People were already buying travel trailers up everywhere for temporal housing.

Finally, she located a brand new travel trailer and a new generator to work with. Susan stocked the travel trailer with canned goods, bottled water, toilet paper, and any other nonperishable supplies she could think of. Dennis left, pulling the travel trailer with four crew members, not knowing what they were about to face. Next to the NOAA location were warehouses full of fish and other seafood rotting in a stench that would take your breath away for miles. None of my crew had ever experienced such horrible and unbearable working conditions before, but they rose up to meet this challenge. They toiled tirelessly for sixteen hours every day until all those units were blocked up, put totally together, and anchored to the ground, just in case Mother Nature might have another horrible trick up her sleeve for this season. We brought the first mobile buildings to the coast after the destruction of this storm.

During a disaster like this, all rules and regulations go out the window. You could pull mobile homes and office buildings for twenty-four hours, day and night, even without wide load permits or routes. For the next few months, that is what we did. We hauled mobile office buildings from every city in our region to every city or town that Katrina had affected. We pulled eighteen hours a day–seven days a week, stopping only long enough to get a few hours sleep, wherever and whenever we could. And yes, Brownie pulled as hard and strong as any of my other trucks!

I wasn't a young man anymore, and I guess I must have thought I was. I pulled from Dallas to New Orleans, and then turned and went straight back to Dallas again. I did this for nearly two weeks, with only a quick nap in the seat of my truck. My son-in-law only lasted for three days on this schedule before he yelled "Uncle" and proclaimed he had to get some rest. I teased him about it but relented and told him to go home for a day or two before returning. My daughter's boyfriend lasted a little longer than he did before he had to take a break. But this old man had never given up or left anything unfinished in his whole life. I kept pulling and pulling until one night, I called my sister in eastern Texas from a truck stop near her and said, "Sis, you've got to come and get me. I can't make it any farther. I haven't slept for two days; pulling these buildings to New Orleans. Will you pick me up? I don't think I can drive one more mile."

Within twenty minutes, she came flying into that truck stop. I knew big sis had a nice warm bed, a good home cooked meal, and most of all, a hot shower at her house. When she got me in her house, she said, "Bobby you look like death warmed over.

Are you trying to kill yourself? Get a hot shower and I'll get you something to eat. Then you are to lie down and rest."

I had a terrible time pulling my boots off. My feet and legs were swollen near double from sitting and hanging them down driving for so many hours. My shoulders burned like they were on fire. When I looked at myself in the mirror, even I was shocked by my appearance. It's a miracle how the Good Lord made up the human body! With a little rest and nourishment (along with nurturing from big sis), I was ready the next morning to start out again.

My daughter's boyfriend took a mobile office down to one of the parishes in southwest Louisiana. Close to dark, he reached a guard checkpoint that had huge floodlights. He had a flat tire on his office, and while he sat on the ground about to change his flat, one of the guardsmen ran over and started waving his hands and yelling. He couldn't imagine what he had done wrong, but he stood up to better hear what he was saying. He was now hollering and pointing, too. He soon realized that he hadn't done anything wrong, but those gators crawling up on the concrete close to him might not know that. Pulling up a little closer to the huge floodlights was immediately his next option. The guardsmen told him that those gators were everywhere, brought inland by the storm. And if he had anymore flats, he might want to check around before laying under the office, especially in the dark. When he got back home from that trip, he told me, "I'm sure glad I didn't have any more flats on that office."

I just laughed and said, "You'd have made a lot of gator bait, big boy."

It was nearly six months after Katrina, but orders were just now coming in to haul offices into the New Orleans area near Chalmette and St. Bernard Parish. This was the area most devastated by the storm closest to the Ninth Ward, where so many human lives were lost. Imagine how I felt: Crossing Lake Pontchartrain on steel runways laid out on the only lane left of this four-lane bridge, with no railings on either side. Looking to my sides, I crept along with my office, seeing nothing but concrete pillars sticking out of the lake, knowing this was where the other part of the highway used to be. It sure crossed my mind and I wondered, *In all these mass confusion, had anyone really checked to make sure that what was left of this bridge I'm rolling on is actually safe for travel?* I'm here to tell you, it was an eerie feeling.

St. Bernard Parish still looked untouched by many hands even six months later when I arrived with those offices. As I came to the south bank of the lake, where the casinos used to be, I saw four-story buildings moved over 150 feet from their concrete foundations, leaning like the Tower of Pisa. I saw a tanker truck hanging out the third story of another building, like it was placed there on purpose.

But while working in Chalmette and St. Bernard Parish, nothing moved and stirred me more than the discovery of human bodies being found six months after this storm. I was working on double-wide offices in bulldozed over Walmart parking lots, where bottled water, sea rations, and equipments were brought in on rail cars and stored by contractors working this area. Chills would run up and down my spine when a huge horn would blare. I had been told by one of the contractors, that it was a signal that another body had been found in the debris. Then in a few minutes, you would hear sirens coming to take the body to wherever they still took them. I thought, *How in our world, with all the resources and technology available to us, could it possibly take us over six months to recover someone's body?* How can all these people stand the pain and heartache of not knowing where their loved one is for so long? I can't even imagine such a travesty in this great nation of ours. I saw a lot of things there which our news media or our government ever reported to the rest of this nation. I am embarrassed by the lack of responsibility our government showed, both locally and nationally, in the aftermath of Katrina. I chose not to tell any more than I have in this story so as not to embarrass officials further. I don't really believe I have been more proud to leave a place than I was New Orleans. I pray that I never have to witness anything close to a Katrina in my lifetime. I also hope that my family, my crew, and I had helped in our small way with our diligence and work to help in the rebuilding of our southern coastal regions.

With Katrina behind us, the next two years were spent mostly in moving mobile office buildings along Oklahoma and north-west Arkansas. Both our leasing companies in Tulsa had contracts to provide classrooms and casino buildings everywhere in that region. It was nothing unusual for Dennis and our crews to setup seven or eight double-wide classrooms in less than a week at the same school. Indian casinos were being built at every corner of the state, and there seemed to be no limit of how much money they would spend on these buildings. Our income for these two years was tremendous. I'm not telling you this to brag about how much money I made. I'm telling you this because most of you reading this book would never have thought that moving mobile home and mobile offices with only three toter trucks and nine workers could create a business that could make over one million dollars per year, especially owned by a man who started from such humble surroundings with so little education.

Chapter Nine
Way Too Much Family in My Business

When you have been in the mobile home business for twenty-seven years and managed to weather it just like all the storms, you are fooling yourself. I had fought the hard reality of just starting out on my own—anxious and ambitious, wanting to be successful. I had gathered thousands of repo mobile homes from unfortunate people who were not able to survive a recession. I had paid my part to decrease our national debt by forwarding thousands of dollars in taxes. I had helped rebuild a part of our nation after a national disaster. I had worked long and hard to help my neighbors in Oklahoma with their growth to rebuild and renew their school systems and Indian casinos. I had dabbled in politics in my state to change a law that made it possible for others in my business to be more successful. But this new and last challenge may be one of the most difficult to face in my career.

All seven children from our blended family have now matured into adults, and each one of them has tried to become a part of this crazy mobile home business at some point in time. My parents were dirt poor and had no way to financially help me get started. They had no knowledge either that there was a better way out there. But I had experienced it and had the knowledge and capability, thank God, to help my children make a better start in their lives.

I'll start with our youngest daughter, Melissa, who worked with Susan, at first, during her summers in high school, and learned every aspect of the business from our office. Susan taught her to cordially answer our phone calls and deal with customers who wanted an estimate for moving their home, then scheduling their move on our calendar, so we wouldn't promise to move someone and not be there on time. She filled out moving contracts and ordered permits for moves. Susan, who hated running around town, eventually sent her each morning to check the mail, pick checks up from dealers, and make bank deposits. Our banker once said, "Melissa is a very smart, intelligent young woman. I believe you have taught her so well about your business that I would trust her to do whatever needs to be done with your banking." After she became pregnant with our first grandson, got married, and then graduated from high school with honors (unfortunately in that order), she worked with Susan in our office for nearly four years. Since she married her first husband so young, both of them not knowing what married life would be with a small child, it soon ended in divorce. After remarrying again and giving us a granddaughter, she worked part time for us while juggling a husband, two small children, and her studies. She eventually graduated as an RN from nursing school.

Our youngest son, Dennis, the only child we raised who didn't finish high school is probably the most like me. When I consented for him to get his GED and quit school, I never imagined he would be such a quick learner in my business and was like a sponge absorbing what I could teach him. He worked long and hard to please the customers on any job I sent him to do with one of my crews. He and his crew probably turn out more work than any crew in this business, and it's always done right, just like I taught him.

After giving my middle son, Johnny, his first toter truck, he only stayed with it about a year and a half. He claimed he couldn't find any good help. It cost a lot to keep the truck in good condition. Insurance was high on the trucks, and he wasn't making enough money. I had heard all this before. He sold the toter truck and bought a used eighteen-wheeler, leasing it to a company that had hauls all over the U.S. and Canada. Eventually, the motor blew up in that truck and he couldn't get all the money to have it repaired. Guess what? He needed to work and started driving another toter truck for me in the mobile home business.

Now, the middle daughter, Christy, is another matter! She is the only one of our children who never really found her niche is my business. She pitched in a few times where needed but never really had much interest in the mobile home business. Susan says she is too much like her real dad. She walks like him, talks like him, and has had as many relationships and jobs as him. She keeps telling us she has issues and is still trying to resolve whatever she thinks those issues are. At thirty five, she needs to find her place in life and go forward, or at least, that's what Susan and I keep telling her! She's a good girl, and we love her. Not everyone can work for us in this business.

Sue's only son, Bud, only worked part time in the business for me that one summer. After the trip to Padre Island, Texas, it was hard to coax him out in the heat again. For the next two summers, he was the activities director at a day care. All the kids there loved him and would run up to him shouting, "Mr. Bud! Mr. Bud! Come and play another game with us." When he graduated from high school, true to his word, he got his college education in business management and has worked for a major equipment sales and rental company ever since. He and his wife vowed to never have any children. They enjoyed going places and doing things with each other too much. But after being happily married for several years, about two years ago, a miracle happened—our twelfth grandchild! I can't be prouder of the kind of parents they are either.

My oldest son, Chris, has helped me off and on over the years since he was fifteen. Chris never liked being hot, dirty, or sweaty. Most days, when he would work with me, he would always have a change of clothes in the truck with him. You can rest assured, if he got too nasty, he would change into them. While working for me, he got a bad Staph infection in one of his knees and was in the hospital for several days on antibiotics. After he was released, he decided he had enough of this business and was certain that the Staph was from crawling around under one of these filthy mobile homes. He got a grant and joined our youngest daughter in nursing school. With two kids of his own, he worked extra hard, even taking on extra classes, so he could also graduate with an RN license at the same ceremony as our youngest daughter.

Stephanie, Susan's oldest daughter, who is about Chris's age, only came to work for us recently in the office to help Susan. She has taken over the same duties that Melissa shared. With two small girls, she and her boyfriend (who had three boys) never seemed to have any money left at the end of the bills. She is friendly and courteous on the phone and fluent with our computer work. It gives Susan a much needed break from all the paperwork.

Now that you know we are family business, let me explain the conflict that comes with that. My son, Johnny, my son-in-law, and my daughter's boyfriend are all driving my toter trucks by now. My son, Dennis, is escorting and setting up homes all over the place. All of them know how much we get paid to move a mobile home. They know because on jobs that they do, they are responsible for collecting the money and bringing it to the office. Sometimes, in a single week, they turn in over 25,000 dollars to deposit. All that each of them sees are those checks, and think I am getting filthy rich! They begin grumbling about getting a raise and needing more money. And each week, one of them questions how much they get paid.

Now remember, my business is B&S Mobile Home Service, and Susan and I are the sole owners of it. I told you I wasn't going to argue with my kids about money, and they all are hard workers and do a great job. Susan and I talked, and then called them in with what we thought was a good solution to stop their grumbling. We formed a subsidiary company with Susan and me owning 50 percent of the stock shares. We gave Melissa and her husband 25 percent ownership, and, our son, Dennis, 25 percent ownership. It was agreed that Susan and I would draw a salary of 3,000 dollars per week, Melissa and her husband and Dennis would draw a salary of 1,500 dollars per week. I had high hopes that with them knowing what their check each week would be, maybe (just maybe) they would quit arguing about money and just work. We also proposed to them that any profits we had at the end of the year would be split with them accordingly. A little later, when my son, Johnny, came back to work, we all agreed to pay him the same salary but with no ownership. Everyone else would be paid by the job like always, including my daughter's boyfriend.

This seemed to quiet everyone down for a while, and we could just go out and work, maybe with a little peace and quiet each day. Then again, this already struggling economy once more reared its ugly head up like a viper waiting to strike. Soon, our work slowed down enough that Susan and I didn't draw a check every week, even though our kids always expected theirs. It was evident that we were in for some tough times again!

People were being laid off from their jobs after many years of service. Major banks were in trouble. Ford and GM were threatening to file bankruptcy if our government didn't help them. You heard all these stories! I know you watched the news as stimulus money was doled out to people in high places who had not managed their money like they should have. A lot of people had made some very poor choices running their businesses, even worse our government had done a much worse job running our nation. People were scared of what would happen. Those who had a little money to still spend were holding on to it. I myself asked how this could really be happening, but I made some decisions that I hope would help my small family business of nearly thirty years remain solvent.

After dinner one evening, as we usually did, Susan and I sat discussing the state of affairs of our nation. We both knew that with a little luck, she and I could possibly weather this new storm. This business had by no means made us millionaires, but we did have a little money we managed to save. Our main concern was how our children and our five employees, who had been very loyal working for us, would manage if they had to go without a paycheck. It might mean they would start asking for us to personally loan them money to pay their debts. I know, as most of you parents know, that when you loan your children money, it isn't really a loan. They believe it becomes a gift never to be repaid. In our case, with the children working for us, at some point, we could take it back as a deduction from their paycheck. But I knew that it would just create more grumbling and arguing with them, and I didn't intend for that to happen.

Our next course of action, at this time, was the best solution I could come up with. Repos were again becoming plentiful in this struggling economy. If we could take some of our personal money and buy a few repos, that would create a few more jobs for our company. It would allow our boys a job to bring them in, a job to clean and repair them, and, when and if we were lucky enough to sell them, a job of delivering them to a buyer. I didn't know at the time if this would work. I decided that unlike other business owners who were just sitting on their money or laying some of their employees off work and trying to hang on, I would try to create more jobs and work for my family and employees until things leveled off more with our economy.

At first, I only had money to buy one or two of these repos from a finance company. As we brought them in and got them ready to sell, I soon realized that this just might work. I began to sell them faster than we could get them ready. Before long, I had money to buy four or five per month, sometimes even more. Then some mobile home dealers in our area complained to the finance company about our purchases. They were jealous of our success, and we were stepping on toes one more time it seemed. We were a transporter, not a licensed mobile home *dealer* in Arkansas. The finance company was supposed to sell these repos only to licensed dealers off a bid list. The representative from the finance company called and said, "Bobby, I appreciate you buying repos from us, but some of the dealers we sell to have complained about you not being a dealer. I can't let you buy any more homes from me. I'm sorry."

This had really been working well for me, and you can imagine my disappointment when he told me this. It was unfair in my opinion, but his position on this was final. To become a mobile home dealer in Arkansas, you had to put up a 5,000-dollar cash bond, have an office with a public restroom, and a sign displaying your dealership name. While in the midst of deciding if I wanted to go to all of this trouble and expense, I ran into a close friend of mine.

This friend had closed down a thirty-year-old established mobile home dealership several years before to go into another venture. Over lunch, we talked about the economy, his new venture, and the mobile home business in Arkansas. I explained to him what I had been doing with repos and how that idea had been shot down recently. He looked over at me said, "Bobby, that's total bull crap. I think I know a way to get around this. I have paid my yearly license fee on Big Three Mobile Homes, and even though it's currently on inactive status, it's in good standing with the Arkansas Mobile Home Commission."

As I listened with more interest in what he was saying, he continued, "How have you been buying these repos?"

I told him, "Susan and I have been using our money that we saved, and we have been able to buy and sell just a few before this happened."

I couldn't believe what he said next. "I would be willing to let you use Big Three Mobile Homes' dealer license if you could use me as partner. I've always trusted you and Susan when we did business together in delivering my mobile homes. And you are both honest and respected business people. We could each put up 15,000 dollars as capital to buy homes with. I still have a sign with Big Three Mobile Homes on it."

Now, he was really getting my attention! I had an office building with a bathroom already on my property. If he was serious, this would work for me!

Within a few days, corporation papers where changed on Big Three Mobile Homes with the Secretary of State's office, showing he and his wife and Susan and I as shareholders of his company. The dealer license with the Arkansas Mobile Home Commission was changed, showing us all as owners, and removed from inactive status to active. We deposited our 30,000 dollars into a bank account to buy repos, and I called the finance company representative requesting a dealer repo bid list. At first, I don't think he believed me, but when I faxed him our paperwork, he had no choice but to send me that list.

With all this happening, I kept telling myself I would make it work. I sure didn't want to *give* my children any money. No one had ever given me anything in this life and my children were no different than I. Except for one little simple thing: they had a Dad and Mom who never gave up. They had never thrown their hands up in desperation and quit. This family business would somehow survive but only through new ideas and extra hard work from each and every one of us!

I'm so proud of the hard work and determination of all our children. They have listened and learned from us and their mistakes in much of the same way I had to when I started this business. But I am even prouder to turn them loose, cut the apron strings, and send them out as responsible, mature adults. I have every confidence they will each be successful in their endeavors, whatever business they end up pursuing!

Chapter Ten
Why I'm Not Quite Done

At sixty-one years old, after thirty years in this business, most of you would think it was about time to retire and enjoy the rest of your life or, at least, slow down. This January, after our children insisted one more time that they need more money, Susan and I decided it was time to throw all of them out on their own. We had a big family meeting and gave them an outline of what our intentions were for them. We thoroughly explained that we could not afford to increase their salaries again. Susan explained that not only did we have a huge payroll to pay each week, but we also had phone bills; office supplies; insurance on all the trucks; truck payments; electricity and water bills; setup parts expenses; fuel each day for the trucks; permits for each job; upkeep, servicing, and truck repairs; and bonds and licenses necessary to run the business. They all nodded their head and agreed that they already knew this, but Susan and I both knew they didn't have the foggiest idea about how much money it really took to run our business. Susan even put it all down on paper to stress to them where our money went, even if it didn't seem to be soaking in to them.

I looked each one of them in the eye as I told them, "It's winter time right now, and somehow I hope that, even with this economy and bad weather, we make it until spring. We have a tough three months ahead of us before our work usually picks up again. I'm tired and I'm going to slow down whether you believe it or not. The time will come to turn you loose on your own, and we have decided that time will be on June first."

That brought smiles to their faces, until I continued to talk. My proposal was that I would sell them each a toter truck for 12,000 dollars, with payments to me at 1,000 dollars per month. They each could decide which escort truck they wanted and would continue to make payments on it until it was paid for. I went on to say that we would split all the hand tools, such as jacks, hammers, saws, and whatever, equally between all of us. They needed to save the money in the next six months for their own insurance, mobile home setup bond and license, operating authority, corporation filings, and enough operating money for at least two weeks.

With this, Dennis looked over at me and asked, "Dad, how much money do you think we will need to save?"

I replied, "A minimum of 5,000 dollars to get started. We chose June because that's when all our insurance renews, and you can have a fresh start."

Now, they had depended on Susan and me to give them a paycheck for as long as we could remember. Not one single week had they ever missed a paycheck from us. They had taken for granted that, each Friday, they could take their pay envelope, rip it open, and run to the bank with a paycheck even though, for weeks at a time, Susan and I might not write ourselves a check so theirs would be good. That was all right with us. We didn't need a paycheck every week at this point in our life. This business had been very good to Susan and I!

Don't think that we were just shoving this idea down our children's throats! All of them at some point—some of them over and over like a broken record—had asked us when we would slow down and turn the business over to them. We had tossed this idea around several times, but until now, we didn't think they were ready to be "thrown out to the wolves" by themselves. Each of them had the work ethics down pat, and they could deliver and setup any mobile home as well as anybody in the business.

As I walked over to get another cup of coffee, I could see each of them looking one to another. I knew, without a doubt, that their minds were racing a hundred miles an hour, and they were trying to process everything I had just said. I walked back over to our table and finished with this sentence, "You don't have to do any of this if you don't want to. But I am not fending for you anymore. I have given you the knowledge to go forth in this business on your own, and I am offering you the tools to make that start. I am not totally quitting. I will retain B&S Mobile Home Service and continue to move whatever repos that I buy and sell with my truck. You will have to form your own companies under another name of your choosing. You can all talk and think about it and let me know your decisions."

Susan and I had already decided that the finance company repo account would remain ours, as well as one dealer account that we also had. Since we had the same phone number for thirty years, we would still be quoting moves every day when people call in on that number to move their homes. To cover our phone expense, pay Stephanie, and our time, they would pay us a hundred-dollar per week booking fee for the moves we would refer to each of them. We told them that we would help them get started by referring these moves, but they would need to get out and hustle some accounts on their own. As they left, we had a good feeling about what we had offered to them, but had no idea what their decisions would be.

The next morning, our son-in-law and our son, Dennis, gave us their answer. They decided to join together and form a company called Boyd and Henley Mobile Home Service. They had anticipated this day for a while and had already saved part of their money for this venture. Our son-in-law would drive the toter truck, and Dennis would drive the escort and help work the crew. They seemed excited to get started and assured us that they would have their money together by June. They were a little anxious about having enough work to make all their expenses, but we assured them that if there was work, they would get their fair share of referrals.

Our son, Johnny, took longer to make his decision. He questioned us about the age and condition of the toter truck we were going to sell him. Since he had already experienced our business once on his own, he knew that used trucks always needed some sort of repairs. Also, still on his mind, was that eighteen-wheeler he had, in which the motor blew up, and he didn't have enough money to pay for getting it repaired.

I told him, "Johnny, it's a machine. That truck is in good shape right now. We've fixed anything that went wrong with it when it happened. But it's still a used truck. I can't guarantee you that it won't break down tomorrow. It's an opportunity I've made available for you. But if you decide not to take it, it's okay. I will sell the truck, it's your decision."

He decided to try our plan, but we ran into a small snag. The toter truck we were letting him have wasn't paid off at the bank, and we couldn't pay it off right now. We agreed to keep the truck in our name and let him continue working for B&S Mobile Home Service until the balance on the truck was paid. He would make payments to us just like the other boys. When the last payment has been made, I would transfer the title over to him. We would also give him referrals, and he would be responsible for all expenses just like it was in his own company. He has done well with this arrangement, and in five more months, he could operate under his own company name. *Then finally,* all our children will be out from under our wings.

These boys have done well with their new companies. We have managed to give them work through the summer and fall months with our referrals. They have handled the pressure of being new business owners well, even pursing work on their own without our help. I believe they will make it in this business and be successful. I will continue to help them with my consultation and knowledge, as they need it and ask, but I will *not* write them a paycheck.

I have continued to buy, sell, and move repo mobile homes for Big Three Mobile Homes. I still pull a few of them for the finance company and store them at our sales lot for other dealers to bid on and buy. Occasionally, when my children's moving schedules are full, I may even move an individual's home from one place to another. I pull homes for my dealer, who has become more like a brother than my very good friend. He has his own setup crew, so I don't have to set them up for him. But I am *not* trying to break my old record of pulling six mobile homes in one day, or pulling someone's home 2,900 miles across the United States.

Our son, Bud, and his wife and Susan and I bought a mobile home park last year. It brings in 60,000 dollars per year before expenses. When we pay off the mortgage at the bank, I'll have a little more income from it. I have some double-wide rental units I setup on the farm here for retirement income, and they're all paid for. Most of those renters have become almost like having family living here. I owner-financed some repo mobile homes for individuals on contracts, and they pay really well. My last toter truck—a big, black "hoss"—is almost paid for. And when it is, I'll be debt free. This truck, I hope, will carry me on to my total retirement, whenever I decided it's that time.

Through the ups and downs of thirty years of hard work, this business has been very good to me, and I have been blessed. My CPA drove my tax return and financial statement out here last year, and I will never forget what he said to me. "Bobby, I've been doing your taxes for nearly forty years. I remember when you were farming and lived in that small twelve-by-fifty mobile home. You own this 100-acre farm, house, and all these rental properties. You have those contracts and your mobile home park bringing in money. Your business is still thriving. You and Susan have accomplished so much. I admire your determination, and I am really proud for you. Do you know you are worth over *two million dollars* now?"

I did not really know that, but I don't count or consider my wealth. I will continue to count the blessings I have been given!

You have followed my story with some interest if you're reading this part! Most of you may be wondering, why don't I just quit and enjoy life? Every day, I meet someone new, and every day, I will have a new story to tell about moving mobile homes. Some of the stories are still funny and others not too funny. Why, as long as I am still healthy, would I want to give up a business that is so much fun and still thriving after thirty years? I am the older son of a sharecropper, with a sixth-grade education from Phillips County, Arkansas. But now, I am also a successful, mobile home transporter. Why would I want to quit?